D1564773

Down the Up Staircase

Tales of Teaching
in Jewish Day Schools

The Jewish Education Series:

Down the Up Staircase

Tales of Teaching
in Jewish Day Schools

Carol K. Ingall

The Jewish Theological Seminary of America

To Josie and Maxie
and the next generation

The publication of the Jewish Education Series
is made possible by the generous support
of Mr. Earle Kazis and the Kazis Publication Fund.

The indexing of this volume was supported by a grant
from the Lucius N. Littauer Foundation.

Cover image: Education Chart
(Livorno: Moses and Israel Palagi and Solomon Belforte, 1846) (NS) E126.
Courtesy of The Library of The Jewish Theological Seminary.

Contents

Acknowledgments

I am deeply grateful to the three teachers who put up with my *noodging* for ten years. This book is their story and a tribute to their eloquence, patience, and honesty. My hope is that their stories will make the path smoother for the teachers who follow them. I also want to thank my colleagues in Jewish education who gave me feedback on much of this material as I tried out various chapters at professional conferences. Through the Network for Research in Jewish Education and in the Davidson School of Jewish Education, I have found a *hevrah* that both nurtures and challenges me.

Jon Mitzmacher helped me collect resources on recent teacher retention initiatives; his expertly annotated bibliographies saved me valuable time and pointed me in the right direction. David Greenberg converted for the computer the concept maps that Suzy, Nehama, and Lynn drew, a task that was far beyond my simple skills. Thanks to Janice Myerson and Leslie Rubin for making my work more lucid and more accessible, and to the Lucius N. Littauer Foundation for graciously funding a grant to support the indexing of the book.

I want to thank the Jewish Theological Seminary for its commitment to Jewish education and for enabling me to join the company of notable authors whose work has contributed greatly to our field. I also want to express my gratitude to my friends and family, whose support meant so much to me during a particularly dismal period. And to Michael, who would have *kvelled*.

CHAPTER ONE
Introduction

Over forty years ago, *Up the Down Staircase* was a must-read novel. Written by Sholem Aleichem's granddaughter Bel Kaufman, it captured the frenzy of an idealistic new teacher battling student indifference, a mind-numbing bureaucracy, and constant shortages of resources and supplies. Three years after its publication in 1964, *Up the Down Staircase* had already become a play (a staple of high school drama classes) and a Hollywood film. The copy I read most recently was published in 1970, the seventeenth edition of the novel, the dust jacket claiming "over 350,000 copies in print." It is still in print. Using memos, letters, and directives from the principal, student comments, and notes between colleagues, Kaufman tells the story of a novice teacher who confronts a harsh reality and then struggles and crashes. On the verge of leaving, she discovers that she has made a difference in the lives of her students. Her idealism is rewarded, and she stays at the embattled Calvin Coolidge High School.

Although Kaufman's hero, Sylvia Barrett, is never overtly identified as Jewish, Calvin Coolidge is a gritty New York high school populated by teachers with Jewish names, such as Sylvia's mentor and colleague, Beatrice Schachter. The book captures the dedication of young Jewish women of the era who, inspired by the image of culture bearer, devoted their talent for nurturing and their love of learning to the young, in hopes of making a personal connection to their students and connecting their students to a life of the mind. In an era when few women considered medicine, business, or law, teaching was the career of choice for the children of immigrant families moving up the social ladder (Lortie, 1975). Using extensive interviews, Ruth Markowitz (1993) corroborates the appeal of public school teaching for Jewish women during the pe-

1

riod from 1920 to 1940 in her book *My Daughter the Teacher: Jewish Teachers in the New York City Schools.*

As Jews became Americanized and the zeitgeist of the sixties urged social responsibility for the "culturally disadvantaged," other-directed goals outstripped the personal goals associated with a "pink collar" profession. In the sixties, teaching in an urban, multi-ethnic school, as Sylvia Barrett did, suggested a commitment to social change, as did registering voters in the South, protesting against the Vietnam War, and picketing nuclear submarine bases. Many years later, the MacArthur Award–winning preschool teacher, Vivian Gussin Paley (2002), reflected on her own motives and urged Jews to join her in teaching in the public schools. In *White Teacher,* she explores the Jewish sensibility that inspired her and the Sylvia Barretts of that era: "It may seem that I am overdoing my comparison of Jewish feelings and black feelings. But I am talking about feeling different. Perhaps coming to terms with one kind of difference prepares a person for all kinds of differences. At least this is the way it was for me" (p. 28).

The public schools no longer offer the status of professionalism or the opportunity to perform a valuable public service for the vast majority of idealistic young Jews, especially women. The reasons for the disaffection are complex, too complex for this study. I will offer a few in a cursory overview. A significant factor is the opening of other professions for women. Another is that we Jews no longer feel the marginality that Paley first wrote about in 1979. Today, Jews are so mainstream, so Americanized, that Madonna can study kabbalah and take on a Hebrew name. The provocative title of Karen Brodkin's book *How Jews Became White Folks and What That Says about Race in America* (1998) suggests a third reason. It illuminates the floundering of the Jewish/black alliance and highlights the diminution of empathy each for the other, threatening the forty-plus years of white Jewish teachers and black or Hispanic students.

The public schools themselves have been under assault. A recent survey of a thousand American adults contacted through Random Distance Dialing indicated that 74% of the respondents would give the public schools a grade of C, D, or F (Rose & Gallup, 2002, p. 43). The failure of well-intentioned reform agendas of the eighties, the battering of the voucher and charter schools movement, the assault from right-leaning institutes like Rand, Brookings, and Hoover, as well as from well-respected education theorists like Ravitch, Finn, Chubb, and Moe have tarnished the luster of the public schools. One of the most outspoken advocates of public education, Gerald Bracey, describes the scene as if he were a war correspondent (2002). Although he refutes the charges of the critics on the right, Bracey substitutes a depiction that is equally disaffecting to young people hoping to become agents of social change. He describes schools staggering under the burden of multilayered bureaucracy, a culture of "teaching to the test" in misguided attempts to promote accountability, and privatization and commercialization (2003).

The idealism of Sylvia Barrett can now be found among the young Jewish educators who hope to become teachers in Jewish day schools. This book is a study of three young women who began a graduate program at the Jewish Theological Seminary in the hopes of finding an arena where their love of Jewish learning, especially Hebrew language, could be directed and where Jewish rituals could punctuate their professional as well as their personal lives. But they were challenged in their idealism and, unlike Sylvia Barrett, failed to pass the test. Within four years of graduation, all three had left teaching in Jewish day schools. Like *Up the Down Staircase*, my study is a multivocal text. Relying on interviews taken over ten years, graduate essays, supervisors' reports, and e-mail correspondence, I began this study hoping to explore the way that three novices understood day school teaching over the course of time. Intrigued by the possibility of concept mapping (Cliburn, 1990; Deshler, 1990; Novak, 1990), I decided to round out my research methodology by having the then-preservice teachers draw visual depictions of the world of day schools, in addition to the oral descriptions they gave me. Each formal interview concluded with the drawing of a concept map. According to Jackson (1990), classroom life is too complex an affair to be studied from any one perspective. My intention was to study the question of the careers of three young day school teachers from multiple perspectives.

While I could have designed my research as a multiple case study, the work of Sara Lawrence-Lightfoot and Jessica Hoffman Davis (1997) in portraiture seemed to give me the tools I needed to understand how Jewish day school educators develop teacher personas. In order to enter the conceptual world of others, it seemed presumptuous not to consult them. What was appealing about portraiture, as defined by Lawrence-Lightfoot and Davis, was the process of working together with the teachers themselves. Lawrence-Lightfoot and Davis, using the language of art, refer to their "subjects." While the term is used in the world of the atelier, it is also the language of the laboratory and, in that setting, conjures up images of passive creatures, animal or human, who are re-cipients of some sort of intervention. I prefer referring to the teachers who inspired these portraits as collaborators. I spoke with them yearly, first as a teacher to students, and then as an older colleague to younger ones, but always as a sympathetic friend.

Portraiture, as described by Lightfoot-Lawrence and Davis, allows a researcher to capture the complexity and ambiguity of this messy busi-ness we call teaching. I relished the opportunity of seeing a career path through the eyes of the teachers themselves. In this type of study, as Lawrence-Lightfoot and Davis explain, "the researcher is the stranger, the one who must experience the newness, the awkwardness, the tenta-tiveness that comes with something unfamiliar, and must use the actors in the setting as guides, as authorities, as knowledge bearers" (p. 43). All of us, the teachers and the researcher, were meaning-makers: the teachers, who, through their narratives, were telling a story (or painting a portrait, to use the language favored by Lawrence-Lightfoot and Davis); and I, the listener, trying to understand that story.

Another source of the appeal was the assumption built into portrai-ture that there is something good here. In *The Good High School* (1983), Lawrence-Lightfoot presents a series of generous, yet even-handed, portraits of schools that are good in very different ways. This is a very different approach from the positivist model that pervades much of the research of science and social science. The scientific or scientific-wannabe literature looks for faults: what isn't working here and why. Portraiture is posited on goodness. Unlike Lawrence-Lightfoot, I did not choose my teachers; they chose me by volunteering to participate in my study. However, I knew from my experience with them as students that all three brought great strengths to their first teaching positions: pas-sion, seriousness, and knowledge. Yet, like Lawrence-Lightfoot, I was determined not to "deify" my collaborators and paint their portraits—warts and all.

I began the study ten years ago, expecting to see these novices move into the realm of experts; I had planned to look at their growth in light of the novice/expert literature. I try to analyze their growth profession-ally in my portraits. I fully anticipated that, like Sylvia Barrett, the three would have their ups and downs, their passion would wax and wane, but that they would make it, if not to expert status, then certainly to ad-vanced novices within a three-year period. But unlike Sylvia, who turned down a prestigious position teaching college students at Willow-dale Academy to stay at Calvin Coolidge High School, "where the kids really need me," my collaborators left to work elsewhere: in Jewish communal work, to begin a brand-new career in nursing, and for motherhood. Instead of a story of idealism renewed, this research chronicles a story of disillusionment and attrition. It is the tale of three talented newcomers who left the field of Jewish day school education shortly after entering it. I am writing this account for teacher educators like me, who might want to examine the preservice programs that we offer our students; for administrators who hire novice teachers and fail to keep them; and for policymakers who fund Jewish day schools as the mainstay of a flourishing American Jewish community.

The Growth of Liberal Jewish Day Schools

It is a truism among educators to speak of education being "situated." To understand the enthusiasm that Suzy, Nehama, and Lynn (pseudonyms) brought with them when they began their studies toward a master's degree in Jewish education and Judaic studies, it is important to review the brief history of liberal (i.e., non-Orthodox) day schools. The ultra-Orthodox always chose to separate their children, but for most of American Jewry, the public school offered the best hope for rapid enculturation. While transmitting cultural literacy, public school teachers were expected to make little Americans out of millions of ragged immigrants, a task applauded by their parents. Weiss (1982) quotes Ellwood Cubberly, a professor of education and former school superintendent, as saying that the task of schools was to "assimilate and amalgamate these people [the immigrants] as a part of our American race, and to implant in their children, so far as can be done, the Anglo-Saxon conception of righteousness, law and order, and popular government" (p. xiii).

Mary Antin's story "The Lie" captures the seeming confluence of Jewish immigrant and American values (Antin, 1916/1965). Her hero, David Rudinsky, is the quintessential teacher's pet on account of his insatiable curiosity, his endless questions, and his hard work. When David questions his right to sing the words "land where my fathers died," Miss Ralston gives an answer that would stir any Jewish immigrant parent's heart:

> David Rudinsky, you have as much right to those words as I or anybody else in America. Your ancestors did not die on our bat-

tlefields, but they would have if they'd had a chance. You used
to spend all your time reading the Hebrew books, in Russia.
Don't you know how your people—your ancestors, perhaps!—
fought the Roman tyrants? Don't you remember the Maccabean
brothers, and Bar Kochba, and—oh, you know about them
more than I! I'm ashamed to tell you that I haven't read much
Jewish history, but I'm sure if we begin to look it up, we'll find
that people of your race—people like your father, David—took
part in the fight for freedom, wherever they were allowed. And
even in this country—David, I'm going to find out for you how
many Jews there were in the armies of the Revolution. We don't
think about it here, you see, because we don't ask what a man's
religion is, as long as he is brave and good. (pp. 581–82)

Antin, herself a Jewish immigrant who attended the Boston public
schools, captures the Jewish worldview of the first half of the 20th century. The universalism, secularism, and middle-class morality preached
by the Miss Ralstons (however idealized in this portrait) were good for
the Jews. The very traditional community (we would call them *haredim*
today) could re-create the *yeshivot* (academies of higher Jewish learning) that they left behind in Europe. For the overwhelming numbers of
Jewish immigrants, the public schools were the schools of choice.

Even during the brief Hebrew Renaissance brought about by Samson Benderly and his followers in the twenties, thirties, and forties, Jewish education was to be situated in the *talmud torah,* the community
school that would meet in the afternoons and on Sundays. Benderly, like
Miss Ralston, saw no conflict between being Jewish and being American. In his essay on Hebrew at the Jewish Theological Seminary, Alan
Mintz (1997) calls Benderly's approach integrationist: "Hebrew culture
could flourish and be enriched alongside American civilization" (p. 91).
Like Rebecca Gratz a generation before, Benderly was a vocal defender
of public education. Both believed that "morality, universal values, pa-
triotism, civics, and critical skills all should be taught in state-funded
public schools to a mixed body of religiously diverse students, leaving
only the fine points of religious doctrine and practice to be mastered by
members of each faith in separate denominationally sponsored supplementary schools" (Wertheimer, 1999, citing Jonathan Sarna, p. 9). Jewish parochial schools were no way to restore the primacy of Jewish
education in Jewish life. Benderly was adamant. "A parochial system of

education would be fatal to [Jewish] hopes for integration" (Winter, 1966, p. 62).

What happened to change Jewish public opinion? How did the Jewish day school come to be when any suggestion of Jewish separatism was viewed as anti-American and tantamount to voluntary re-ghettoization? Why did Benderly's dream die? As with any educational question, perhaps any question that emerges from social science, the answers are multilayered. There are a number of factors involved. The emergence of the State of Israel, the crisis of confidence in public schools and concomitant growth of educational privatization, "white flight" from the centers of Jewish settlement in large metropolitan areas, ethnic pride after the 1967 Israeli war, economic success, and the triumph of Miss Ralston's dream—that is, the fading of a sense of marginality*—have all contributed to the rise of Jewish day schools. In addition, the suburban synagogues demanded schools of their own, schools that were often bar/bat mitzvah factories, competing with soccer and ballet for after-school hours. Benderly's vision shriveled as hours of instruction were pared away. After completing a study of the religious practices of American Jewish adults, Himmelfarb (1975) took aim at the minimalist nature of Jewish education of those who had attended Sunday schools and afternoon Hebrew schools. Turning the tables on the paradigm we have encountered of the nurturing Jewish teacher and her multi-ethnic, multiracial students, Himmelfarb entitled his paper "Jewish Education for Naught: Educating the Culturally Deprived Jewish Child."

Beinart (1999) notes that Jewish day schools could only come to be at a time when Jews were thoroughly comfortable as American Jews and Jewish Americans. Enrollment in Jewish day schools has surged since 1965. Wertheimer (1999) notes that student populations in these schools have tripled since 1962. One observer notes that the increase in day school enrollment (excluding the ultra-Orthodox community) in the 1990s was 12–15% (Schick, 2000). At least eighty new all-day Jewish high schools opened in the 1990s (Avi Chai Foundation, 2000). PEJE, a consortium of funders committed to Jewish day school education, has invested approximately $16,000,000 to the field and contributed to the

---

*Jews have apparently been very attentive pupils to the message of the Miss Ralstons. Fishman (2000) notes that Jewish and American values have "coalesced," blurring any distinction between the two. For those resisting this coalescence and looking for Jewish community and values, Jewish day schools represent an alternative.

opening of more than sixty new Jewish day schools. The National Jewish Population Survey (NJPS) of 2000–01 claims that 29% of Jewish children between the ages of six and seventeen have attended a Jewish day school or *yeshiva,* compared with 23% of adults between the ages of eighteen and thirty-four, 12% of adults between the ages of thirty-five and forty-four, and 7% of those forty-five and older (PEJE, 2000; Geffen, 2004, p. 30). More and more parents have been choosing day schools for their children.

Day schools were suddenly "hot." The boom in day school enrollment commanded the attention of Jewish teacher educators in North America and that of Federations and family foundations. The documentation of soaring intermarriage rates and the apathy, if not antipathy, toward Jewish concerns unveiled in the 1990–91 NJPS caused community leaders to look to day schools as the "silver bullet" of Jewish continuity. The expanding number of day schools and the promise of full-time employment encouraged a growing number of young people to consider day school teaching. Suzy, Nehama, and Lynn saw themselves as Miss Ralston's successors, bringing Jewish literacy and values to the latest claimants of the label "culturally deprived," their fellow Jews. Like Israel Friedlaender (1907/2004), my respondents were troubled by the question of "de-Judaization." Reflecting on the success of the descendants of the European immigrants, they, too, worried about the next generations. What would they be "a quarter of a century hence? American? Yes. Jewish? Perhaps" (p. 8). It is for this reason that they chose to begin a graduate program in Jewish education.

Novices and Experts

Besides commitment to a cause, what else characterizes new teachers? In a longitudinal study of four elementary school teachers over an eight-year period, Levin and Ammon (1996) create a typology of teacher development. They identify two early stages in the evolution of a beginning teacher. The first is what they refer to as "naïve empiricism," the belief that teaching is about behaviors that one can learn from watching others teach. Stage two is "everyday behaviorism": embracing the notion of "practice makes perfect," the new teacher is certain that after a requisite amount of time, she, too, can master these behaviors. Beginning teachers simplistically believe that teacher efficacy is rooted in what teachers do. They think much more about teaching than about learning. Kagan (1992) complements this view of teaching as learned behaviors by describing understandings that new teachers seem to lack: what their pupils can do (what is typical for students of this age) in cognitive, social, and behavioral terms; the role of context (from class to class and school to school); and problem-solving skills related to both planning and instruction. Kagan reminds us that teaching is about more than behaviors; it is about thinking. It is also about technical skills and practical knowledge. She makes the case, as do Ammon and Levin, that the thinking of veteran, skilled teachers is far more complex and multidimensional than that of novices.

One of the most thorough explorations of how experts differ from novices can be found in Bransford, Brown, and Cocking's *How People Learn: Brain, Mind, Experience, and School* (2000, p. 31). They note the following characteristics, which I have summarized below:

1. **Experts notice features and meaningful patterns of information that are not noticed by novices.** This key difference is also identified by Carter, Cushing, Sabers, Stein & Berliner (1988); Carter (1990); and Copeland, Birmingham, De Meulle, D'Emidio-Caston & Natal (1994). Experts can "read" their students and classrooms much more quickly than novices can. They have a body of lore, know what's typical, and can interpret and devise solutions based on "internalized templates" (Carter et al., p. 29).

2. **Experts have acquired a great deal of content knowledge that is organized in ways that reflect an understanding of the subject matter and of the learners.** This is what Shulman (1987) calls "pedagogical content knowledge": an amalgam of content knowledge and what works with whom, when, and where. Feiman-Nemser (2003) calls this "situationally relevant approaches to subject matter" (p. 26). Wilson (1991) gives examples of this skill within her field, the teaching of history. Not only do experts need to know their subject matter (history) in a detailed manner, but they also need to know the other disciplines that constitute the social sciences. For Jewish day school teachers, this would mean not only knowing biblical narratives in order to teach *Tanakh* but traditional biblical commentaries, contemporary research done by Bible scholars, the history and archaeology of ancient Israel, as well as how Jews and others have read the Bible over time. Wilson would expect an expert history teacher to know how to transform the subject matter for the

learner and how to evaluate curricular materials in history (or, in our case, Bible) critically.

3. **Experts don't see isolated facts or propositions; their knowledge is "conditionalized."** By conditionalized, Bransford et al. refer to the experts' tendency to organize their thinking around core concepts, or "big ideas" (p. 36). Borko and Shavelson (1983) refer to these cognitive structures as prepositional structures, schemata, or scripts. Using these key concepts or conditionalized knowledge, experts can then help to organize learning for their students.

4. **Experts can retrieve information fluently and flexibly.** Like Schoen (1983) in his classic research on the reflective practitioner, Bransford and his colleagues note the artful, seemingly effortless, way the expert can adapt his or her craft to the rapidly changing kaleidoscope that is a classroom. While Schoen refers to what virtuosi seem to do instantaneously as "reflection-in-action," Bransford et al. refer to automatic and fluent retrieval (p. 44). Fluency can be seen in the way that an expert reads the mood of the class and changes his or her direction accordingly. Weinstein (1989) points out that an expert can do certain things quickly and elegantly, while a novice is barely able to "read" the scene, let alone react to it. "A good teacher is more than a willing worker with good intentions. . . . [T]eaching requires imagination and the ability to orchestrate activities in an unpredictable, complex environment" (p. 59).

5. **Experts have adaptive expertise.** Novices know when a class "bombs," but it takes them longer to read the signs of faltering attention or lack of comprehension. Experts not only read the signs quickly, but they have a repertoire of remedies to employ. In addition to solving problems that affect their students' learning, experts can apply this skill to their own learning as well. Unlike novices, they also know what they don't know and can use what they do know in new situations (Bransford et al., p. 48).

Sternberg and Horvath (1995) suggest another view of the expert teacher. She has knowledge that cuts across a number of domains: content knowledge, problem-solving knowledge, organizational knowledge ("big ideas" around which she organizes what she knows), and knowledge of students and contexts. In addition, she has what Polanyi calls tacit knowledge: "the knowledge one needs to succeed that is not explicitly taught, and that often is not verbalized" (Sternberg & Horvath,

p. 12). In addition to having acquired knowledge, the expert is efficient; she can solve problems more effectively than can a novice, as well as faster. Last, according to Sternberg and Horvath, the expert has insight. She can come up with more creative solutions to the problems that she faces and can recombine what she knows in more creative ways. In her study of a beginning teacher, Stark (1991) quotes a promising beginner who understands that teaching demands self-reflection:

> I saw teaching as a mode of *doing* rather than *being*. I saw knowledge as a commodity collected during teacher training, and pedagogues as people who passed this knowledge on to students. I did not see pedagogy as a personal encounter between myself and others, nor did I critically examine my assumptions about being a teacher or about education, knowledge, learners and society. (p. 294)

Lily Chin, an expert teacher whose portrait has been limned by Cohen (1991), demonstrates a set of qualities that are more about heart than mind. She speaks of her temperament: "I was born under the sign of the rabbit," referring to her ability to adapt (p. 52). She also displays a passion that does not appear on the list of the cognitive theorists. This passion is for her subject, biology, and for collecting materials that she can use in her teaching. Chin's enthusiasm remains after thirty-two years teaching, although it has been tested by rampant student dishonesty, state and district budget cuts, mind-numbing "professional development," and an appallingly low salary. Even great teachers, after years in the field, consider leaving. In her study of twelve expert teachers, Williams (2003) reveals that eight of them had actually quit and returned (p. 73).

"Time on task," a classic concept in educational theory, cannot guarantee expertise. But experience—and thinking about that experience (metacognition)—builds on the domain knowledge learned in school and on the job. Johnson (1989) calls this amalgam "embodied knowledge." It is that personal, practical knowledge that is crucial to professional success. It is "knowing how" and not just "knowing what" (p. 375). When combined with the resilience of a Lily Chin, embodied knowledge not only defines experts, but it also keeps experts teaching.

Feiman-Nemser (2003) sums up what new teachers need to learn. Her findings complement the literature on expert teachers:

1. **Situationally relevant approaches to subject matter** (pedagogical content knowledge).
2. **Standards and expectations of the school and district.** While Jewish schools do not deal with mandatory curricula and testing in Judaic studies, novices still need to learn "the way we do things there."
3. **Crafting a teaching persona.** Cary Grant is said to have confessed, "I pretended to be somebody I wanted to be, and finally, I became that person. Or he became me." Novices seek the efficacy and agency that experts have, play-acting until the masks they wear become their faces.
4. **"Nitty-gritty things like transitions and momentum"** (p. 26).
5. **The ability to size up situations and to know what to do.**
6. **Teach as a member of a professional community, within a school culture** (p. 27).

Learning these things takes time. In her interview with David Berliner, a leading researcher of teaching expertise, Marge Scherer (2001) reminds her readers that it takes five to eight years to begin to master the craft. If 40–50% of new teachers leave before five years (Stone, 1987; Perez, Swain & Hartsough, 1997), as did Suzy, Nehama, and Lynn, they leave before they can savor the sense of accomplishment and pleasure that experts derive from their professional success. Through their reflections on their teaching, both in verbal and nonverbal form, my collaborators discuss the experience of their preservice education, their induction into the culture of day school teaching, and their early years of day school teaching. I have written this book in the hopes of understanding why these three left the profession that initially seemed so compelling to them. I wanted to know why they, with so much to offer, took the down staircase past the mezuzah and out the schoolhouse door, while others, albeit all too few, manage to climb up from the ranks of beginners to become master teachers.

CHAPTER TWO
Suzy: The Search for Safe Havens

When I first met Suzy,* she was in her twenties, a petite, slender woman with a big smile. She spoke quickly and laughed easily, using her hands to punctuate the conversation or to brush a wayward strand of blond hair from her face. Her speech contained traces of the American South, where she had spent many of her formative years. An accomplished student, she sprinkled her conversation with references to books and articles that helped to define her thinking on education. Rav Kook, Philip Jackson, Howard Gardner, and Samson Raphael Hirsch appear not as pedantic flourishes but as touchstones for her musings. Reflection seemed to come easily to her, although she understood that introspection sometimes takes time. Discussing a painful episode, she observed, "It was one of those scenarios where I thought, okay, there's probably an opportunity to learn something here from this, but it's not going to be clear until after I get out of this year, until I'm faced with it again" *(interview, 1994)*. The fact that she seemed comfortable with metacognition buoyed me as a researcher. Suzy seemed to love to talk; interviewing her was always easy.

Suzy grew up in the South and the Southwest. Her mother, a social worker, met her father, a surgeon, in the summer camp that they attended as teenagers. They settled in small Jewish communities as he pursued his medical training, eventually landing in a city where there were professional opportunities and extended family. When she was in the third grade, Suzy went to a Jewish day school for the first time. She

---

*All names of students, administrators, and schools in this study, with the exception of the Jewish Theological Seminary, are pseudonyms.

studied until grade seven in two different day schools in the same community and remembered her day schools as places that made her feel comfortable and content. Although her parents were very involved in their synagogue and community, they worried about the quality of the general studies in the middle school of the local day school and reluctantly sent her to McCord, a prestigious private school. Suzy recalled McCord with ambivalence:

> It was liberal education at its best. I had PhDs teaching me. I studied religion and philosophy. It was a great school, so that's the only reason that I stayed there because for me, the school— ironically, as social as I am—was not a social outlet a lot of the time. I just could not relate to a lot of those people. Their biggest worries in life were if they had enough Louis Vuitton bags. *(interview, 1994)*

In a conversation with a group of preservice teachers, Suzy related a defining moment in her McCord education. Three or four students near her were drawing swastikas. The teacher saw them and did nothing. At that point, Suzy decided that she would make purposeful Jewish choices to find Jewish environments where she could feel at home.

Suzy continued her Jewish education through high school by attending a Jewish school one day a week, an experience that she remembered with great fondness:

> I really loved the times when I was back with my day school friends in religious school. I was definitely starved for Jewish companions. We lived in a Jewish part of town, but I was so busy with school and after-school sports and this, that, and the other. . . . It was such a present that I got. . . . We went just on Saturdays, so we couldn't write, but the classes were as relevant to our lives as possible. Most of the time, we had really cool teachers. Because we didn't write, we had one class, we'd have services, then we'd have another class, and it was a very laid-back atmosphere. Most of the time, kids didn't skip class because the class itself was discussion-oriented . . . so it was social and, at the same time, educational. It was great. Not everyone ranted and raved about it as much as I did, but I was also in a very disciplined, formal type of environment during the day at school, so to me, this was great. But for my friends who were at public school, it wasn't

as much of a treat for them, because they were with each other during the day and then came on the weekends, too. So to them, it wasn't as big of a deal, but for me—I loved it. *(interview, 1994)*

Attending a summer camp that brought together Jews from small towns and those from big cities all over the South was another formative experience. The camp director was one of her heroes, someone who "saved a generation of Southern Jewish kids" *(interview, 1994)*. Denominational boundaries did not loom large in Suzy's life. She attended communal day schools, a Conservative religious school, a Reform camp, a Conservative graduate school, substitute-taught in a Modern Orthodox day school, and taught for three years in a Conservative day school. What was most important to her was her feeling of being most at home with fellow Jews. This realization drove her choice of a college, yielding an acceptance from one with a large percentage of Jewish students. "My mother said that when I got into Lovell University, it was as if I had died and gone to heaven" *(interview, 1994)*.

While at Lovell, Suzy visited Israel during her junior year. There she participated in a JESNA (Jewish Educational Services of North America)-sponsored internship in Jewish education. Upon her return for her senior year, she volunteered in a Jewish day school and in an organization that helped victims of domestic abuse. A chance conversation with the Hillel rabbi directed her to the Jewish Theological Seminary and a master's degree in Jewish education. Commandeering a napkin from the cafeteria, he plotted out a career path for her. Suzy confided that she had saved the napkin among her memorabilia. Coming to New York was a treat. Suzy had always felt marginal as a Jew in the South:

I had no idea that I was going to like it here [in New York] so much. I knew that it was kind of like the [Jewish] Mecca. It's culturally and socially acceptable to be Jewish. I had never felt that way before, even at Lovell. I have a Jewish star that I have literally not taken off since the summer of '89 when I bought this [showing me the necklace] at Baltinester Brothers in Jerusalem. . . . There were way too many instances in the South where I kept it tucked in because I didn't know how people would react or what people would say. I didn't feel comfortable enough. And I do up here. It's just so different the way that it feels. You can express yourself. I went to a housewares store at the beginning of the school year, and my Jewish star happened to be out, and the manager there, not Jewish, wished me a happy new year. I mean, it just blew me away. *(interview, 1994)*

As much as Suzy loved New York, in the JTS dorm she once again experienced the marginality that had characterized her years at McCord. Assigned to a suite with a number of rabbinical students, she found her religious practices scrutinized and found wanting by one of her more zealous roommates. This roommate made Suzy feel inauthentic as a Conservative Jew. Suzy sorrowfully recalled her discomfort:

> It was very disheartening to be in a Jewish environment and feel so on the outskirts because I went to a WASPy prep school where I, for sure, was made to feel on the outskirts, but I didn't mind because I didn't really want to fit in to their world. But again I found myself in a world that I didn't necessarily want to fit in to, but [this time] it was my own religion. *(interview, 1994)*

The thrill of being in such a Jewish city, where *Simhat Torah* was celebrated so openly ("dancing in the streets with Torahs"), didn't compensate for Suzy's feeling that she kept failing the halakhic tests of dorm life. Her food didn't have the requisite *hashgahah* (rabbinic supervision); her phone rang on the Sabbath. It was not until her second year, when she took an apartment with a like-minded friend, that she hit her stride both academically and socially. This was the year in which Suzy did her student teaching, which, in retrospect, Suzy judged to be more about Suzy learning her cooperating teacher's routines than finding her own teacher voice. However, Suzy did learn that she had a knack for easing her students' anxieties. The following is from a self-evaluation she wrote as she finished her semester of student teaching:

> Finally, the area that I feel most confident about in reference to my teaching experience is my ability to work effectively with the children. An example that demonstrates this is an incident that took place on *Yom Ha'Shoah*. Shlomit had told the children some of the history of World War II and the impact it had on Jewish life, but she did not focus on the killings. Ari, one of our kindergartners, came up to me afterward to tell me that his grandparents had been in the Holocaust and that he was really sad. I pointed out that he was lucky that they survived. He said

something to the effect of yes, it was great that they lived, but even those who lived were really dead. I was shocked to hear such a comment from a six-year-old. I realized that he had obviously overheard such a comment in his household. So I remarked that though they might never forget it [the Holocaust], I was sure that he makes his grandparents happy to be alive. Hearing that comment, he smiled and ran off to play with the other children. (final self-evaluation, 1996)

Like most novice teachers, Suzy began student teaching determined to meet the affective needs of her students (Weinstein, 1989). One of the important lessons that Suzy learned in her practicum was how difficult it was to attend to children's individual needs and still be cognizant of the needs of the group. In her interview after she completed student teaching, Suzy mulled over this challenge:

I think one of the things I need to work on is finding a balance and a diplomatic way of saying, "I really do want to hear what you have to say, but I need to get through this." I think that I've gotten better, but I definitely noticed that I was so idealistic, believing that every kid has a voice, and every question is a good question, and every comment deserves an ear, and so on. But sometimes, other kids in the classroom were rolling their eyes because they were tired of listening to this child talk. It really had nothing to do with what we were discussing. *(interview, 1996)*

After receiving her master's degree, Suzy, unlike her classmates, opted to postpone entering the world of work. She decided to go to Israel to study in an *ulpan* and perfect her Hebrew. Never one to resist a challenge, Suzy held herself to a high standard. She was concerned about her Hebrew fluency. Could she be hired as a member of a Judaic studies faculty in the kind of school to which she aspired? She might be able to get a job teaching Judaica in a day school elsewhere, where standards were lower and desperation greater, but she was determined to meet the expectations of the more demanding New York day schools. Therefore, shortly after graduation in 1996, Suzy went off to Jerusalem, where she studied Hebrew through February 1997, returning to engage in a job search. As she interviewed in various day schools, she sharpened her skills by substitute teaching in a Modern Orthodox day school. She was

eventually hired by her first choice of schools, a brand-new day school
that made a point of breaking down the artificial boundaries between
Judaica and general curricula. Suzy was thrilled:

> I didn't want to be pigeonholed. The administrators might ask,
> "Are you interviewing for general or for Judaic?" and I'd say,
> "Well, I'd really love the opportunity to do both, if at all possible."
> That wasn't really possible in a lot of places. I figured that even if I
> did the Judaic, after a while I'd want to be involved in more than
> just that. If I did the general, I'd be missing the fulfillment that I get
> out of teaching the Judaic. I really lucked out because there was a
> place that was created. While I was gone, it got off the ground. I'm
> very committed to being a Jewish American. *(interview, 1997)*

Torah im Derekh Eretz
(Jewish Learning and General Education)

Integration of the particularities of Jewish life, culture, values, and practice with the world of general culture was always a robust theme in
Suzy's conversations. It is part of her personal practical knowledge, as
Clandinin and Connelly define the term: a distillation of her past and
present experiences that resonates throughout her stories of herself and
her teaching (1996). While a student at Lovell University, Suzy participated in a study experience in Spain that combined Jewish history with
trips to the Prado and other jewels of Spanish culture. In a paper she
wrote during her first semester in graduate school, she discussed the appeal of multiple intelligences theory:

> Because of the integration of Judaic and secular studies, in addi-
> tion to community involvement [Suzy is referring to parents
> playing a part in the life of the school], *cultural dissonance be-
> tween what goes on inside the school versus what goes on out-
> side, as well as dissonance between Jewish and American
> identities is diminished."* (1994; italics mine)

Britzman (1986) notes the importance of the preservice teachers'
"implicit institutional biographies" in shaping their attitudes toward
teaching. In the case of Suzy, her attitudes about integration were a reaction to her institutional biography: the discomfort she felt as a student
at McCord; the bifurcation of her Jewish and American identities as a

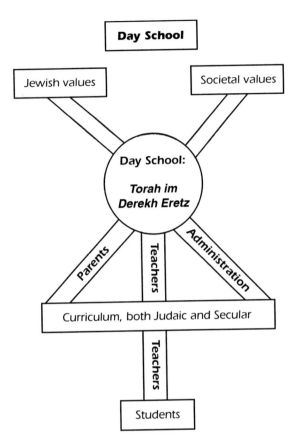

Figure 1

Southerner; and the compartmentalization of knowledge in the day schools that she attended, the one in which she student taught, and the one in which she did substitute teaching.

Suzy's earliest concept map (Figure 1), drawn after one semester of graduate school and before student teaching, depicts two streams of information, Jewish values and societal values, channeled into one pool, labeled "Day School: *Torah im Derekh Eretz*." Interpreted by parents, teachers, and administration, this pool becomes the stuff of a bicultural curriculum. Suzy then thought in terms of two disparate, finite bodies of knowledge, which somehow, in the hands of the adult authority figures in the school, would be magically transformed into curriculum. (This "somehow" evolves over time, becoming clearer in each of Suzy's maps and interviews.) Her discomfort with the "separate but equal" approach to education emerged more clearly over time. During that first year of preservice education, while discussing her first web diagram with me, Suzy noted that her theory classes reflected a similar, artificial division. She was taking courses in Judaica and in education. They weren't integrated. "To a certain degree, I'm approaching my studies as if they were two separate things" *(interview, 1994)*.

After her student teaching, Suzy's criticism deepened; she referred to what she observed, one teacher teaching Judaica and one teacher teaching general subjects, as comparable to children engaging in parallel play:

> I think Judaic teachers need to have an interest in their children's progress in their secular subjects, and vice versa. I think that there should be a conscious integration—even if the teachers teach in separate rooms: "What are you teaching today? Oh good, I'll mention that in relation to my history lesson about such and such." You know, there are so many ways to send messages to kids that take so little effort, but you just need people, good people, to do it. We need principals who care about goals like this. *(interview, 1996)*

Suzy suddenly became aware of the unheralded partner in Jewish day schools, the teacher of secular subjects, and her potential as a Jewish educator (Pomson, 2000).

> The secular teacher, a teacher who may not even be practicing but who is very committed to the idea of teaching general subjects within a Jewish environment, can have as much effect on a child's Jewish identity and on the Jewish lens through which he or she sees the world as a Hebrew teacher can. *(interview, 1996)*

While still a student, and without ever seeing an alternative, Suzy had come to the conclusion that day schools as usual were not for her. The bifurcated model, half the day devoted to Judaic studies and half the day devoted to general studies, seemed artificial. Her reflections on what this curriculum might look like can be seen in her second concept map.

Suzy has discovered embedded learning, the importance of context. At the center of the map is her latest iteration: Jewish and Secular Education in a Jewish Environment. The bifurcation of knowledge is replaced by bilingualism—subjects are taught in Hebrew and English.

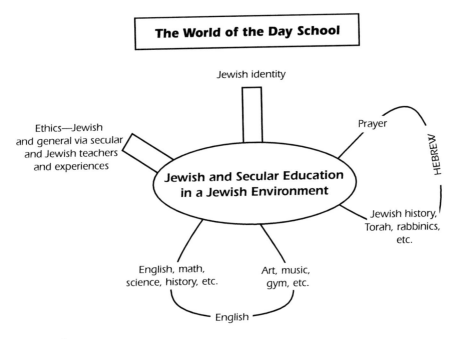

Figure 2

However, Jewish knowledge cannot be separated from general knowledge. Epistemologically and pragmatically, they are commingled. (Note Suzy's discussion of ethics as one domain, Jewish and general, "via secular and Jewish teachers and experiences.") The Jewish ethos of the institution suffuses all that transpires under the aegis of the school, helping to shape Jewish identity. But Suzy was still a prisoner of the "deep structures" of schools. Jewish and secular learning may not exist in separate compartments with impermeable boundaries, but curricular subjects are still very distinct. There is prayer, art/music/gym (what schools call "specials" or "specialty subjects"), English, math, science, history, and so on. When I asked her what her ideal day school might be, Suzy tried to reimagine what she had come to know and question while a student and a student teacher:

> I think that the day school has a lot more than just Torah and the ways of Torah to offer its children. It's not a sprinkling of secular subjects. It's a true integration of American culture and Jewish practice, culture, and ideology. *(interview, 1996)*

The Day School

EDUCATION — *marching to the beat of the Jewish calendar*

School Philosophy

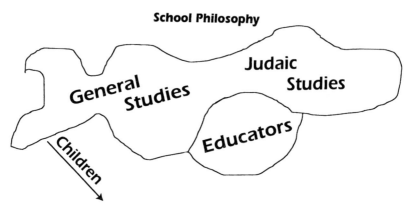

Figure 3

Unsure of what true integration was and how to make it happen, Suzy resolved to find something different, which was bolstered by her study in Israel (including performing American plays in Hebrew) and some time to think about day school education. Upon her subsequent return to the United States, where she substitute taught in a very traditional day school, she was sure that there had to be another way of thinking about curriculum and organizing day school life. Both Buchmann (1987) and Kagan (1992) note the importance of dissonance in forcing a novice teacher to confront and modify her personal beliefs. Suzy was meeting that dissonance head-on, creating a third concept map that was at direct odds with the two previous ones.

Gone are the channels, circles, and neat rectangles. Suzy produced what she humorously called "the blob," or "the amoeba." In this concept map, knowledge is not contained in closed boxes labeled "Judaica" and "General Studies," "Torah" and "*Derekh Eretz.*" Knowledge is sinuous and fluid, co-constructed by children, parents, and teachers. It consists of general studies and Judaic studies, but they are unbounded, floating in a sea labeled "Education—marching to the beat of the Jewish calendar," a reflection of the school philosophy. Suzy, thrilled to be hired by a new school that promised to break down the barriers be-

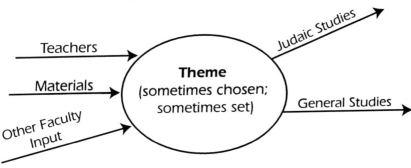

Figure 4

tween Torah and *derekh eretz*, anticipated what she hoped to find in her first real teaching position in a day school. Her words picked up speed and tumbled over each other as she described the school whose faculty she would be joining in the fall of 1997:

> In the school that I'm going to teach in next year . . . there can be a math workshop going on at the same time that something else is being taught in Hebrew, and it's in the same classroom, and both teachers are Hebrew speakers, and both teachers are connected to Judaism and have, you know, pretty extensive knowledge, so it's just, it's just, it's almost like electricity, like this constant flowing thing. There's no real separation between . . . there's not a switch, you know, for half the day and then, you know, another switch for the rest of the day. *(interview, 1997)*

That first year of teaching presented a number of challenges, to use one of Suzy's favorite words. One enormous challenge was how difficult doing real integration was. The children chose themes to study that interested them; the task of the teachers was to draw in the various content areas: math, science, language arts, Hebrew, and Judaica around the theme. Drake (1993) refers to this type of integration as transdisciplinary, building a curriculum around a theme that might open up inquiry in various disciplines. Suzy stated:

It's really hard when these kids say on Friday that what they want to study is the rain forest, and then over the weekend, on Sunday, you have to run around to public libraries and all the other stores you can think of, pulling together a unit that will be interesting and informative and that you can work into math and science and writing and Hebrew. It's just a lot of work. *(interview, 1998)*

Reflecting on the struggle to meet the challenge of doing real trans-disciplinary integration, Suzy's concept map, drawn after the completion of her first year of teaching, deals solely with the curriculum (Figure 4). Gone are the lofty ideological frameworks, the concern for the construction of knowledge as an enterprise engaging parents as well as teachers and students, the importance of nurturing Jewish identity. Suzy was exhausted by what she had to do with limited resources and time. She was simply trying to survive. Stark (1991) describes two teachers whom she studies during their first year of teaching. Like Kim, Suzy was caught up in a technocratic vision of what teaching is about. It was about the doing of the job, rather than what Stark calls "being in the world" (p. 303). When asked to depict a day school, Suzy brought her most recent institutional experiences to her drawing: the day school was defined by the relentlessness of the theme chosen by the children. The theme propelled all life in the school, controlling Judaic studies, secular studies, teachers, materials, and other faculty members.

Suzy's last concept map (Figure 5), drawn at the close of her second year of teaching, returns to her theme of *Torah im Derekh Eretz*. She smiled when I pointed out the tenacity of this concept in her philosophy of education and remembered when she first heard the term at Lovell. "I remember thinking that I don't care if it's Orthodox; it still speaks to what American Judaism is. You have to modernize, but still maintain. . . . I still believe that" *(interview, 1999)*. By the end of her second year of teaching, Suzy's frenzy over creating curriculum *de novo* had abated. Once again, her peripheral vision returned. She had overcome the Sisyphean challenge of pulling together these child-centered themes. She could see beyond the rock that she had to roll up the hill. A Jewish day school was also about a board, administrators, and teachers, operating in a culture shaped by parents and the wider educational community, working together to shape a curriculum promoting cultural literacy and values. An ideal day school presupposed the primacy of children and honored their individuality.

Day School Education

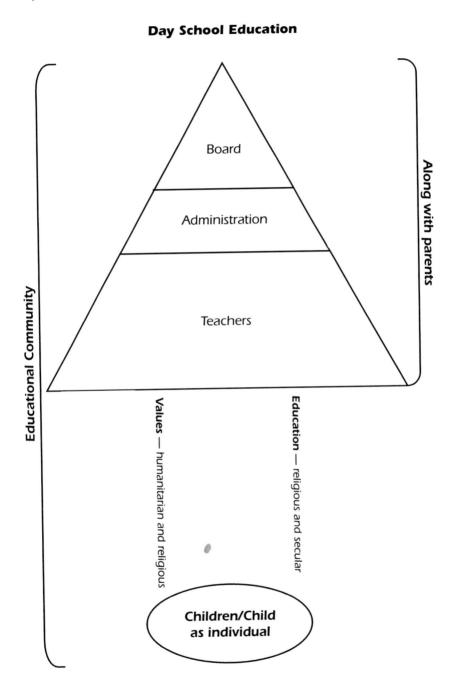

Figure 5

"Flying by the Seat of Your Pants Every Day"

Constructivist pedagogy was a natural complement to Suzy's philosophy of Jewish education. Over the course of the first five years in which we spoke, her commitment to a student-centered pedagogy grew. From her first papers written in graduate school, when she wrote about multiple intelligences and their potential role in a Jewish day school, to the interview we conducted after her third year of teaching, she sprinkled her conversation with words such as "meaningful," "empowering," and "challenging." The definition of an implicit theory as provided by Clark and Yinger (1977) is "a reflective, socially derived interpretation of that which the teacher encounters and then serves as a basis for the actions she constructs" (p. 295). Like *Torah im Derekh Eretz*, constructivist pedagogy was one of Suzy's implicit theories. Like the Bourgeois Gentilhomme, who didn't realize that he was speaking prose, Suzy didn't know that she was a constructivist. What she did know was that there had to be an alternative to what she called the "binary mold" of Judaic studies and general studies and an alternative to frontal instruction, where "the teacher is . . . doing everything and handing everybody the same piece of paper" *(interview, 1998)*.

Elbaz (1991) reminds us that implicit theories do not emerge fully formed. They are nonlinear in nature. Although Suzy used a "new paradigm" vocabulary in her first interview as a graduate student, vestiges of the "old paradigm" showed up in her first concept map. In that concept map, the one she drew upon the completion of her first semester (Figure 1), after she had read Gardner and Perkins and had written a paper on multiple intelligences, she still drew students as a box into which knowledge would be funneled. (In one of our later interviews, when we reviewed all the concept maps, Suzy pounced on this early depiction and covered her face in mock embarrassment.) But after student teaching, study in Israel, and a semester of substitute teaching, Suzy used the word "facilitators" instead of "teachers" and crystallized her thinking about teaching and power. Unlike Britzman's novice teachers, Suzy resisted the language of control, enforcement of rules, and teacher as teller (1986, p. 445). She spoke about the primacy of learning, not teaching, and how teachers mistakenly plan with their own needs, not those of their students, in mind. "What I now realize is that [the planning process] was so much more for the teacher to feel like she was teaching than for the kids to really be learning" *(interview, 1997)*. The year before, sounding much more like a novice, Suzy had commented on her disappointment that graduate school didn't include helping her with classroom transitions, with moving students from one activity to the next. In the spring of 1997, as a substitute teacher, Suzy understood that there was no way that graduate school could have prepared her for all the unpredictabilities of school life. She reflected on what had transpired that day in her classroom:

> There's a lot that comes with experience. I had to accept that as being true. There's no way to control for. . . . I mean today, for example, a fifth-grader of mine came up to me telling me that she had fallen in the mud during recess, and her underwear had gotten dirty. How would you ever have planned for dealing with issues like that? So how are we going to get them clean? How are we going to get her a new pair? Et cetera. I mean, it's those kinds of things you would never discuss as a class, being a student of education, and that's just a typical pragmatic example. There's just a lot that you just could never plan for, as many classes as you have on behavior management. (interview, 1997)

She continued on the issue of teacher power:

> They say that all teachers have a little bit of a control freak in them. Maybe I just thought, "I have to be doing so much more for this to really go well." Some things flopped, and I've now internalized the idea that some things just flop. I don't think I was willing, as a first-year teacher, to let that happen. It happens. It's really scary when you feel like everything's on the line for a particular lesson, and if it flops you feel like a failure. Whether or not it's because they just came down from recess or [something else] . . . you never think of the compounding factors. That's the one thing, if there's any one thing, that I can take away from this experience at this school. . . . I really owe it to [the students], because I feel like it's even going to make me a better mom; it's not just for this scenario. [Teaching in a day school] really has to do with just listening to children better. (interview, 1997)

Britzman's teachers cling to the belief that teaching is all about them—that "unless the teacher establishes control there will be no learning, and, if the teacher does not control the students, the students will control the teacher" (1986, p. 449). Although a novice, Suzy had a far more sophisticated notion of control. She already shared ownership of the curriculum with the students. They chose a theme, and she scurried to deliver an artful and challenging unit around their interests. This is what she called "flying by the seat of your pants every day," running to libraries and bookstores to accommodate her students' curiosity while weaving in the various subject domains around the theme. In the review of the literature on experts and novices compiled by Cushing et al. (1992), the authors note that advanced beginners and novices talk about management and control, while experts use a language that underscores the interactive nature of instruction. Experts speak of learning, while novices speak of teaching. Suzy, who used this language even before she took on her first real job, was now bolstered by the culture of her school in her resolve. Even after her first year, she was beginning to speak like a seasoned professional.

Suzy also learned a second important lesson during her first year. It, too, deals with the nature of control. What Suzy discovered is that not everything that the teacher plans succeeds. No matter how well crafted the lesson, no matter how many intelligences are tapped, learning takes place in a context that the teacher cannot always control: before lunch, when students are hungry; after a fight during recess; and with children who may be experiencing problems at home. Suzy realized that being a successful teacher meant developing an extra set of ears to tune in to children's readiness to learn. And even with an extra set of ears, lessons still might fail.

As sophisticated as Suzy's thinking was about issues of power, teaching, and school life at such an early stage in her professional career, there were times when she did seem to fit the typical pattern of novice thinking—for example, in imagining schools to be far less complex than they are (Weinstein, 1989). In her first four concept maps, there were no signs of school boards and the importance of lay leaders in setting policy (and limiting teacher control; see Figures 1, 2, 3, and 4). By the end of her second year of teaching, she had a "crash course" on the influence of the board on school life, especially in a new school. This distinction appears on her fifth concept map (Figure 5):

> There is a sort of hierarchy of decision making in a lot of different realms, because, for instance, we're still in a temporary place because [the school in its fund-raising efforts] didn't raise enough money. There are a lot of things that are out of our hands. I felt that the control starts with the board; the administration is a sort of second tier. We're sort of under the administration. I wrote a little bracket [around] "along with parents"

because there are parents who are involved at all these levels. *(interview, 1999)*

When Suzy used the expression "flying by the seat of your pants," she was referring to the pressure of creating curriculum *de novo*. However, given her observations about living with the uncertainty of school life, this description seemed to encompass far more than curriculum design.

"You're Never Totally Ready"

In her discussion of the cultural myths of novice teachers, Britzman (1986) notes three prevailing assumptions: everything depends on the teacher; the teacher is the expert; and teachers are self-made (p. 449). In her analysis, "everything depends on the teacher" is a statement of the need for teacher control. Suzy did not sound like a Britzman novice by her second year of teaching. She accepted her limited power and the inevitability of "flying by the seat of [her] pants." Just as she had recognized the fact that she would never have total control, she accepted the fact that she need not be the sole expert in the classroom. As early as her first interview, she acknowledged how much children know: "Just watching these kids pull from the knowledge that they already have, but learning more—it is always so exciting" *(interview, 1994)*. All these understandings bode well for Suzy's movement along the continuum from novice to expert. Fortunate to find a school that provided a professional culture that seemed to match her implicit theories, Suzy felt that she had found a nurturing context in which to try out her views on teaching and learning:

> The kids at my school are so empowered from the time they walk through our doors. . . . I have to say I mean *everything*—[both the curricular and the cocurricular activities]—empowers them. There's a morning meeting, and instead of the teacher leading it, there's a student leader for the week. The child reads the schedule and calls on people if he or she needs help. The students vote on themes. The power is really up to them. *(interview, 1998)*

When I asked Suzy about the high point of her second year of teaching, it was about the children turning to one another for help rather than to her. "My children rely on themselves, and then rely on each other, and then I'm the third person that they turn to" *(interview, 1999)*. There was no need for her to be the sole source of authority in the classroom.

Suzy seemed comfortable living with ambiguity and imperfection. Expertise is not only shared; it is also elusive, just out of reach. Suzy would not suddenly awake one morning to find that she had been magically transformed into an expert. She was in the process of becoming a constructivist educator, a process that would be lifelong. Suzy looked like an expert-in-the-making. She reflected on the head of the school and how he led discussions with kindergarten children on the meaning of prayer:

> Dr. Strong pushes the kids an extra step more than I would. He asks much harder questions, and it's amazing to watch. It's only fifteen minutes, this discussion, twice a week, but it has made me a better teacher just by watching him in action, by observing the way he thinks and the way he says, "But why? But why?". . . He always thinks of that extra something. So that's one instance where I sit back and think, "Oh, God. I have so far to go."

Suzy's professional identity and her religious identity were evolving. There was no sudden illumination, no magic elixir, no silver bullet. She seemed to grasp the idea that teacher knowledge was a process, not a product. In clarifying some of the details of her religious journey, we had the following exchange:

> CKI: After you moved out and moved away, you said that you felt that you had approached some kind of middle ground . . .
>
> Suzy: . . . which I still think I'm finding. . . . *(interview, 1996)*

From her student teaching days on, Suzy felt that good teaching was a journey, not a destination. "It's as if you're never totally ready. You're never totally seasoned. You're never 100 percent competent in every step that you take. I think it's the same with teaching or with Judaism." There was no formula. Suzy refused to buy into the cultural myth that teachers are born, not made:

> I learned a whole lot in my classes in terms of the education. I took some at Teachers College at Columbia, which were very helpful, and I took a lot at the Seminary that were extremely helpful in terms of opening up my mind to different ways of approaching children. Even looking at the career not as a job but

as something that you really develop. You're not expected to be an expert at the very beginning; there's a continuum. Another benefit—and I don't know if this is a Jewish thing—is that I have always felt, and I was made to feel at the Seminary, too, that everything was just a taste. There's still a lot to learn. I really appreciate that sort of philosophy because I'm always—if I can afford it—going to be taking classes and improving my point of view, my knowledge, and the way that I approach children and interactions with parents. *(interview, 1996)*

"There Have to Be Havens"

If Suzy didn't sound like one of the novice teachers depicted by Britzman (1986), she did sound somewhat like the teachers studied by Weinstein (1989). Like them, she spoke far more about students' self-esteem than she did about achievement (Weinstein, p. 54). To be sure, Suzy did speak of achievement. After her first year of teaching, I asked her, "What made you feel most like a teacher?" Her response was, "The kids have really internalized a sense of 'Oh, I'm an author' by age five, and 'I read books,' and then 'I read with a partner' [they coach each other], and 'I can help people now, and I couldn't at the beginning of the year' " *(interview, 1998)*.

But Suzy was far more passionate about the issue of emotional climate, and the language of emotional well-being was far more pervasive than the language of academic achievement in her interviews. The crisis of her first year of teaching was feeling left out, ignored, and even disparaged by her co-teacher, while being let down by the administration. In Ryan's stage theory of teacher growth (1986), the first year is supposed to be the fantasy year. Suzy's dream of finding a community of teachers that was a community of learners was dashed. She felt that she was struggling alone. She discovered how difficult it was to integrate curriculum, to make *Torah im Derekh Eretz* a reality. But the biggest shock was to her self-esteem.

> The kids were difficult. My co-teacher was difficult. The parents were difficult. I felt as if my supervisors didn't really support me or respect me. You know, things like that. I also felt the overarching issue was that I really lacked confidence, and there weren't many aspects of my experience last year that enabled me to build up any sort of real confidence. *(interview, 1997)*

A leitmotif in Suzy's biography was the need to feel comfortable in her environment. She longed for the feeling of comfort that she had experienced at her day school and at her religious school, that she felt when she came to New York and didn't have to whisper the word "Jewish" in public any more. The teacher as caregiver and the school as a haven were some of Suzy's strongest implicit theories.

During her third year of teaching, Suzy butted heads with the administration over her concern for Josh, a kindergarten child who suddenly lost bowel control. In discussing the situation with his mother, Suzy discovered that the child's home life had undergone a significant change. The administration thought that Suzy was playing therapist and accused her of failing to maintain appropriate boundaries.

> I didn't really know who was right and who was wrong. I was playing the role of a social worker or psychologist or something. That's my natural tendency. . . . We are talking about the whole person here; we're not just talking about how many books the kid can read. However, I felt as though I was very much put in my place, and [told to] like really remember my job, my role as that of educator rather than psychologist or social worker. That was a huge source of cognitive dissonance for me this year. Like, what am I doing in this field if that's not what I'm here for? Because for me, that is why I'm here. (interview, 1999)

In retelling the story, Suzy tried to be evenhanded, giving the administration its due. But later in the interview, she dropped the veneer of objectivity:

> A lot of the staff are single women. We can pour every ounce of ourselves into this [teaching]. . . . I mean, I do all my lesson plans on notebook paper. I don't know; maybe some people sit at night and type it up on the computer. People choose to put their efforts and energies into different things. Mine was the kids as people. And you know, if caring is a crime then I'm a felon. I mean, so that's kind of how I felt. So arrest me! Arrest me for caring! I mean, I didn't care any more about the boundaries. I felt like no one was advocating on this child's behalf. No one really fully understood how [his home life] was affecting him. (interview, 1999)

In describing the incident with Josh, Suzy used terms such as "privy," "retention," and "letting it all come out." I pointed out her choice of phrases, and we both laughed:

> All I know is that this kid was fine up to a certain point, and something hit this kid in a way that he couldn't handle. I didn't see why getting mad at him and making him feel that where he does go eight hours a day was not a safe haven for him, either, was the answer. You know? There have to be havens. I was thinking about this, you know. My graduate school experience was pretty devoid of havens, but there were certain people with whom I felt okay and [who] made me feel okay. . . . The bottom line is that everybody needs that, and this kid obviously could not speak with his mom about precisely what was going on, and at school he was letting it come out, no pun intended. *(interview, 1999)*

Suzy had discovered a similarity between herself and Josh, and in doing so, understood a good deal of her intensity over the incident:

> I never thought about the parallel of the way [the administration] treated me last year versus the way they handled me and this scenario this year with this particular thing, but it's very similar. Josh was being blamed for something that was happening to him, and that is exactly what happened to me. *(interview, 1999)*

Johnson (1989) reminds teacher educators of the need to pay attention to teachers' embodied knowledge. Suzy's concern for the social well-being of her students was a prime example of that knowledge, a belief that emanated from the way she constructed her own reality. It emerged from her own lived experience and played out in the classroom "through [its] embodiment, with all its tempos, moods, patterns, and projections" (p. 372).

The Day School: "A Vehicle through Which to Teach Values"

Just as the teacher as caring adult remained a constant throughout Suzy's interviews and artifacts, so did the theme of teacher as moral educator. A sociology major in college, Suzy punctuated her teacher talk with words such as "identity," "enculturation," and "community." Three of her five concept maps dealt explicitly with moral values (see Figures 1, 2, and 5). One of the reasons she loved the camp that she attended as a child was that she studied prayer in English for the first time, "learning the values behind the texts I was being taught in day school" *(interview, 1994)*. When I asked her, early in our series of interviews, why she was thinking of making day school teaching her career, Suzy replied:

> I still feel really strongly if you give people background knowledge, a connection that runs deeper than just an experiential one-time thing, they will have something to come back to. They will have something on which to build their Jewish identity. I feel really strongly about the day school being a vehicle through which to teach values. I really feel like in a public school, this is sociologically speaking, it's almost too idealistic to think that you can incorporate values because you can't assume that the values that you'd want to teach or that the school mandates that you teach . . . are [what] the parents want their kids to be learning. I just feel like in the guise of the day school especially, you have traditions, texts, etc. through which you can teach values. . . .
>
> You're training a person; you're preparing them for life in addition to the actual substantive stuff. *(interview, 1994)*

The following year, her second in graduate school, Suzy expanded on this theme:

> I believe, as I've said before, that one of the reasons I've opted for Jewish education is precisely because our tradition provides us with a moral code that under the auspices of *a Jewish day school,* we can invoke and authoritatively utilize!! (self-evaluation, 1996; punctuation and emphasis are Suzy's)

Just as Suzy's approach to nurturing was a reaction to her feeling marginalized during her schooling, so was the primacy of community-building in her definition of moral education. Her priorities were those of Nel Noddings (1992): maintaining a climate of caring, establishing relationships, and nurturing respect for others and their opinions. Hers was the feminist voice of moral education. As she remembered her high school, a paragon of academic excellence, she found it a moral wasteland. Although McCord had an honor code, as far as I'm concerned, they did nothing in the way of moral education, nothing in the way of real community-building, nothing in the way of building tolerance. I think a lot of the sort of xenophobia that many of the people at my school have—and it's a problem in the South in general—was simply just overlooked on the part of the faculty because it's bigger than . . . their perception of it. It comes from the home. This all sounds like Columbine High School or something [the immediate response to the shootings at Columbine was an indictment of the shooters' parents]. Does it come from the home? Does it come from a peer thing? Who knows? But I think that they did not feel that [moral education] was a part of what they were being paid for or part of what they needed to educate for. *(interview, 1994)*

After spending a year teaching kindergarten, Suzy was most proud of her accomplishments as a moral educator. "I get them when they're like fresh, wet behind the ears, whatever the expression is. I don't want to say they're like clay and I got to mold them, but to a certain degree, at least, I was able to mold them into a community" *(interview, 1998)*.

Had Suzy been teaching a grade other than kindergarten, she might have spoken more about academic achievement. But her greatest pride was how kind the children were to one another. In looking at long-term teachers, Williams (2003) notes a common element in the thinking of experts. She observes that they focus on the reward of watching students grow, often satisfying their need for a collegial community in their schools with the community they create in their classrooms. Once again, Suzy's teaching persona had begun to represent that of the experts in the literature.

Suzy and I discussed the concept of moral agency as she was about to graduate. What was her source of moral authority? Was it *halakhah* (Jewish law), or autonomous choice based on rational decision making? In answering my question, Suzy displayed the personalism that is characteristic of so many contemporary American Jews, even religiously observant ones (Cohen & Eisen, 2000):

I very much believe in the spirit of Torah and the spirit of Jewish law, but in terms of the letter of the law? That doesn't have as much meaning to me as a person because life is too short to walk around and everything being an obligation. I just have no desire to live my life that way. It's not that I shirk responsibility in Judaism or that I ignore aspects of it on purpose. . . . But that I definitely, I wanted to be able to say at the end of these two years [in graduate school] I do what I do because I have knowledge and because I've made an informed decision. That was another one of the goals for myself in addition to getting skills to go out there and do something with myself in the real world and not just have to get a job. . . . I wanted to be able to be an informed Jew and make choices for myself that felt right because I was choosing with knowledge. *(interview, 1996)*

During her semester as a substitute teacher, Suzy had learned what it often takes novices far longer to learn—that she was not the students' friend:

I think I felt that it was really important that the children like me and thought of me as a friend first and foremost, before a teacher. I think being a sub has sort of given me a different perspective in that I've realized the position of teacher. I don't mean having all this power and sole authority, but being able to get things accomplished, laying down rules without worrying, "Oh, my. Are they not going to like me?" I think that was really important for me to see and to experience because I still have relationships with the children but I also feel like their teacher, if that makes any sense. *(interview, 1997)*

Suzy understood that "the position of the teacher" included being a moral example. She brought it up herself as she struggled with her religious identity as a graduate student, referring to her tendency to ask what her actions would convey to others and what kind of exemplar she wanted to be. She was delighted to be hired by a school that expected her and other faculty members to be *dugmaot* (role models), although Suzy referred to this along with all the other expectations that felt crushing during her first year of teaching *(interview, 1998)*.

In our fifth interview, I returned to an issue that Suzy had mentioned in her first interview: do religious schools have an edge on secular schools in the teaching of morality? During our first discussion, Suzy commented that day schools were the best route to instill and nurture moral values. Although she would like to believe that values could be taught elsewhere, in public or private schools without a religious base, there was no consensus around which values should be taught. Five years later, and after two difficult years in a day school, Suzy's response was more tenuous:

> I think so [that religious schools do have an edge on secular schools in the teaching of morality], but I do want to believe, idealistically, optimistically, that there is a way to accomplish this without religious tenets. . . . I think Judaism is wonderful, and I think it's beautiful because that's also who I am as a person. I have a religion that does speak so much about how to treat human beings. I would think a school like Palfrey [a New York school with a strong ethics program] can probably accomplish a lot without the use of real religion. *(interview, 1999)*

Support from the Administration

After three years of teaching and steady development along the continuum from novice to expert, Suzy decided to leave day school teaching. I knew that she had been having some difficulty, but I was still surprised. I had spoken to her off and on during that year. I had learned that younger teachers on the faculty were turning to her for advice. We had even spoken of the possibility of her becoming a mentor for student teachers in the near future. After all this *nachas*, I was enormously disappointed when she announced that she needed "to take a break." During that third year she had become ill, and the demands of teaching in the constructivist atmosphere that she initially embraced became even more overwhelming to a person exhausted by a glandular disorder. Suzy found the beleaguered administration, still struggling with issues of school survival, emotionally unavailable. This day school, for all its strengths, was not a haven for her; she needed nurturing as much as her students did. She felt unappreciated and unsupported. Suzy did not leave Jewish education altogether; she found a position working on educational policy issues for a large philanthropic agency. But as she explained her reasons for leaving to me in a telephone conversation, her comments after her first tumultuous year seem to apply:

> I decided first and foremost that what makes or breaks your school year, at least with a novice teacher, is support from the administration. If support is lacking, it really sets you back

> months and months in terms of your own confidence, your own
> skills, and your ability to put a lesson together, a unit together,
> in order to work with your co-teacher more effectively. I really
> felt that [support] was lacking. *(interview, 1998)*

Like the teachers Kagan (1992) studied, Suzy discovered several
things: that her initial beliefs and conceptions were unfounded (e.g., creating child-centered, theme-based curriculum *de novo* was enervating, not
just energizing; working closely with a co-teacher could create tension,
not harmony); that she needed more technical know-how (she was ill-pre-
pared for the rigors of planning curriculum); and that she had to create
new ways of categorizing experiences (so what if your lesson fails?) and
new dilemmas (an administration that did not support her as she hoped).
Her preconceptions demanded that a school be nurturing, for teachers as
well as for students. When she found that the school was unable to provide that climate for her, she left both the school and day school teaching.

Epilogue

Suzy walked out of day school teaching at the end of her third year a
self-described "burnout." The classic text on teacher attrition is called
Burnout: The Cost of Caring (Maslach, 1982). Suzy's crisis with Josh,
the encopretic child, elicited her *cri de coeur*, "If caring is a crime, then
I'm a felon." That event was the tipping point for her; her language was
that of someone who had been pushed too hard. She wrote to tell me
about her new job once she was ensconced:

> I realized, when cleaning out my box today, that I never sent you
> a description of my current position. . . . I work with grant recip-
> ients to expand, improve, alter, and evaluate their initiatives in
> Jewish education. (We sponsor an initiative, not necessarily every
> aspect of the institution.) I'm a consultant of sorts. . . .
>
> With regard to final thoughts on day school education: I feel
> that the day school, as an institution, has enormous potential for
> impact on a child's Jewish identity. But many factors must be in
> place for the environment to be rewarding for everyone. The
> teachers need support, the children need teachers who are sup-
> portive and well-trained, and every school must be mindful of

the varying needs of all of its populations. Needs include psychological needs (support for issues that children are dealing with and multiple administrators for teachers to utilize) and financial needs (teachers need to be compensated, especially for the work they do that extends beyond the school day—family ed, writing Purim *spiels*, etc.). I could go on and on; I'm sure you're aware of that. In essence, it's *haval* [too bad] that the intrinsic rewards of being a Jewish educator, after several years with the best of intentions but the "wrong" environment, aren't enough to retain even the ones who "really care." I feel a bit like Rodney Dangerfield for saying this, but as a day school teacher, "I didn't get no respect!" Or, shall I say, not enough to keep me there.

It took leaving the scenario and stepping back from it to understand that it doesn't have to be that way, but who knows if I'll ever venture back to try it again? (e-mail correspondence, August 27, 2001)

She hasn't, to date. Within a year or so in the organization, Suzy began to work with young adults, doing programming, a modest amount of fund-raising, and what she calls "doing adult Jewish education through the back door." (It is interesting to note that Biklen [1986] observes that even though they leave teaching, seasoned teachers' "internal conceptions of themselves as teachers" still remain [p. 506].) Suzy's description of what she enjoys about the position sheds light on what was missing in her day school teaching experience:

I've had a wonderful springboard for a career—all unplanned, all through the back door. You don't know where your life is going to take you. This is a job that is a nexus of my knowledge of content, interpersonal, communication, and organizational skills. And I've found a mentor in the workplace. From the beginning, she communicated what the expectations of the job were, she'd praise me and cc her supervisor, she advocated for me. She increased my responsibility and rewarded me for achievement. It boosted my self-esteem and gave me a vote of confidence. It was a real motivator. I had my mentor's appreciation and the organization's appreciation. The higher-ups noticed!

Stone (1987) focuses on the power of hope and praise as key to retention; Suzy's source of those two powerful nurturants in her present position was a supportive mentor who made sure that Suzy knew what was expected of her, unlike the preoccupied administration in the day school in which she taught.

Validity in qualitative research can be measured by whether respondents answer an interviewer's question in much the same way over time. In our most recent interview (by telephone, 2004), I asked Suzy how her experience might have been different. She quickly came up with a list of responses that I've summarized below:

1. **Lack of support.** First on her list of responses to my question about what would have made a difference was her sense of being stranded. "If the administration had been different. . . . Each administrator had different strengths, but I didn't get much from either. There was no one to go to. It was scary. . . . The administrators were preoccupied; they didn't have any support staff for the kids or for the teachers. There was no psychologist, no learning specialist." Once again, she tells the story of Josh, with the same level of exasperation that punctuated her rant four years earlier.

2. **Unpredictability.** "In this start-up school, the policies were all in flux. We were in borrowed space." This, too, is another factor leading to a culture that fails to make teachers comfortable.

3. **A rough first year, made more so by colleagues.** "I had a particularly difficult class that first year—that class of oddballs." Suzy points out an educational truism: novice teachers often get the most difficult classes. Then, too, her co-teacher was less than willing to rely on a "greenhorn" to plan and implement the teaching. "Co-teaching is so hard. When it's good, it's very, very good, and when it's bad, it's horrid." In the profile of Margaret O'Bryan, entitled "The Rookie," Ryan quotes her as saying that it was the "p" words that got to her: paperwork, people, programs, and politics (1992, p. 2). The "p" words tripped up Suzy as well and highlighted a problem in the school culture.

4. **Lack of materials.** Suzy's concern is often mentioned in both general and Jewish education as a reason that novices leave the field. See Public Education Network's report *The Voice of the New Teacher* (2003) and Schaap (2002). The problem is particularly acute in Jewish education, a profession that is just beginning to create attractive classroom materials.

5. **School philosophy.** "Then there was the ideological rigidity: two languages, curriculum driven by the kids, no recycling the material

we used from year to year, while the administration insisted on teaching everything in Hebrew and even speaking to me solely in Hebrew." In a start-up school, one trying to define its niche in the competitive day school market, the administrators were themselves novices, trying to adapt their school vision to parents who appeared at the schoolhouse door with different agendas.

6. **A loss of belief in herself and in her vocation.** "I was exhausted. I kept thinking, 'I can't stay on this sinking ship.' I was done, spent. I kept imagining myself as a candle with a wick on both ends, burning down." Both Houghton (2001) and Williams (2003) comment on the need for teachers to feel a sense of personal and professional efficacy in order to stay in the field. Suzy had lost faith in her own agency as a day school educator.

I have referred to hope as being central to the worldview of teaching (Stone, 1987). Herbert Kohl (1998), the great progressive educator, entitled his autobiography *The Discipline of Hope: Learning from a Lifetime of Teaching*. So, ever hopeful, I asked Suzy if she could imagine herself ever going back to day school education, to which she replied:

If I were ever to go back, it would be if I were guaranteed enough power, resources, and authority to change the climate for the teachers. I would never have left if I had had that support. My universe was so bad.

CHAPTER THREE
Nehama: "A Time to Dance"

When I first met Nehama, in an introductory class in Jewish education, I could imagine her as a high school cheerleader. Her athleticism and energy suggested the dancer she once aspired to be: not the willowy, classical ballerina, but the sturdy practitioner of folk, jazz, or modern dance. Her shiny brown hair bounced as she spoke; her eyes twinkled; she smiled frequently. She paused thoughtfully as she answered my questions, and when she responded, she did so emphatically and enthusiastically. At our first interview, she volunteered that although she was still unsure of her career plans, she was leaning toward day school education. Her application to the JTS program had indicated that she was headed in that direction.

Nehama grew up in metropolitan New York. Her parents divorced when she was two. Two years later, her mother a married a man who was a paraprofessional with a local Board of Education, who, for all intents and purposes, became Nehama's father. His dedication to education (he went back to school to earn his bachelor's degree) served as an inspiration for Nehama. Nehama's mother, a lawyer, was a product of an Orthodox upbringing.

> We always had a kosher home. My mother grew up Orthodox. When she first married she covered her hair, went to *mikveh* once a month, the whole nine yards. So when she remarried, that completely went by the wayside. *(interview, 1994)*

Nehama attended an Orthodox nursery school and a Schechter day school from grades kindergarten through eight, an opportunity not afforded to her twin siblings, born after her mother's marriage to her step-father. The twins were unable to attend for financial reasons. Finding the advanced Hebrew classes tedious and difficult (her classmates were almost all native Hebrew speakers) and wanting to be "mainstreamed" (Nehama's word choice in her 1994 interview), Nehama refused to attend an Orthodox *yeshiva*, her only day school option. A public high school seemed much more appealing to her, but there was the question of continuing her Jewish studies. "I really wanted nothing to do with Jewish education, but my parents said, 'Go to *Prozdor* [a two-day-a-week supplementary school]. You have to go one year. If you hate it after that, we'll talk again, but you have to go one year.' And I went, and I graduated" *(interview, 1994).*

Besides providing an out from a full-time Jewish education, the public high school offered opportunities to study dance. The opportunity to major in dance was the reason that Nehama chose to attend Western State for college. But soon after her arrival, she decided that neither a dance major nor Western State was for her:

> As a child and through high school, I did a little of everything: ballet, tap, jazz, and modern. I never actually danced at Western State. I only spent a year there and decided at freshman orientation that I really didn't want to spend the rest of my life dancing. I had reached a point at which I needed either to dedicate my time and my life to dance to make it a career, or I needed to do something different. I found myself at a huge university with many opportunities and felt that if I danced, I could not take advantage of it all. When I went to Shoreham [a school noted for its Judaic studies program], I did some jazz and modern dance in a club called Dance Masters. I codirected a dance concert for the club during my senior year. (e-mail correspondence, 2001)

Once she transferred to Shoreham, Nehama majored in Judaic studies. At the urging of a friend, Nehama attended Camp Ramah and loved it; she became a counselor, then a unit head, and acquired a taste for administration. After college, she came to New York to study Jewish education. During the ten years I've known Nehama, there have been many changes in her personal life: an engagement, marriage, her husband's decision to change careers, and the birth of their three children.

The search for community played a significant role in Nehama's thinking about Jewish day schools, just as it had for Suzy. Nehama currently lives in Westwood, a suburb nicknamed "Little Jerusalem," for its abundance of kosher restaurants, synagogues, and day schools. She loves the town. That quest for comfort began early in her life with her decision to transfer to Shoreham University. "I needed a more cohesive Jewish community. . . . It was a Jewish community I was searching for" (interview, 1994). As a junior in college, she participated in the Shoreham Jewish Education Program, teaching in a Sunday morning religious school originally designed for the children of Shoreham professors. Nehama spoke passionately about her career in Jewish education and her concern for maintaining Jewish tradition:

> The words that popped into my head are "promote Jewish continuity." I want these kids to know the stuff so that they can become more involved in their religion and their community and then not intermarry and not fall apart from the center. (interview, 2000)

Nehama sounded like a poster child for the Jewish continuity initiatives engendered by the NJPS (National Jewish Population Survey) 1990–91 report. She aspired to be a culture bearer to the "de-Judaized," to use Friedlaender's (1907/2004) term, or that descriptor borrowed by Himmelfarb, the Jewishly culturally deprived (1975). The young teen who wanted to end her Jewish education at age thirteen discovered a vocation through informal Jewish education after she had become involved with USY (United Synagogue Youth, affiliated with the Conservative movement) and Camp Ramah.

> *Nehama:* [Ramah] was one of the most valuable educational experiences that I had. Many of the kids involved in USY are not very knowledgeable. They come from very secular homes, didn't go to day school, and I had the Hebrew knowledge and synagogue skills that enabled me to get very much involved. I knew that it was from Schechter that I had these skills. So I wanted to, in some way, give back what I had gotten, because it was so valuable.

CKI: All right, but you're describing yourself as a kid who at thirteen said, "I've had it."

Nehama: Right, but a few years later I realized that I began reaping some benefits from it [Jewish education]. It was very easy for me to catch on. . . . My family didn't focus on Shabbat so much; we didn't go to shul. There were no intense Shabbat dinners. I didn't know Shabbat *z'mirot* [Sabbath songs]. I learned all that Shabbat in USY, and I was able to learn it as quickly as I did and appreciate it as much as I did because of my foundation in Hebrew. *(interview, 1994)*

For Nehama, the best way to strengthen American Judaism was through day school education. She wanted to give back what she had received from her schooling: that connection to the Jewish community. The tie consisted of two intertwined strands: competence in Hebrew and the skills to participate knowledgeably in Jewish ritual life.

My brother and sister did not go to a day school and until recently did not get any kind of intensive Jewish education. I wanted to somehow see to it that every Jewish child got a Jewish education. Obviously, that's a very idealistic view. That's not going to happen, but I wanted to do what I could to insure [*sic*] that. *(interview, 1994)*

Like Suzy, Nehama is an optimist.

"And Men Must Walk, at Least, before They Dance" (Alexander Pope)

Nehama began graduate work in Jewish education in 1994. Unlike the novices in the research literature on general education (and many of her classmates), Nehama never complained about her courses in education concentrating on theory at the expense of practice. Britzman (1991) notes that student teachers place great importance on practicing pedagogy while devaluing learning about teaching in the academy. Nehama, on the other hand, seemed to enjoy the balance of Judaica and education, the academic study of Jewish education and the world of teaching. "The theory was essential, I think. It's a basis for teaching. The skills class, just how to write a lesson plan, is crucial. Developmental psychology is also crucial" *(interview, 1996)*. She also loved the internship that she spent at the Board of Jewish Education, where she could combine what she learned about curriculum and instruction with existing resources for Jewish teachers. When I noted that what she was really saying was, "Hey, the theoretical is terrific . . . ," Nehama interrupted and finished my sentence, as she would often do: "And the practical is terrific" *(interview, 1996)*.

Student Teaching:
Warm-Ups and Stretching

Just before she began to student teach, Nehama reflected about what she brought to the experience:

> Among the various strengths that I bring to my teaching lies one that I feel will contribute most to my future success in teaching, i.e., my commitment to the material I teach. My subject is Judaism. To teach Judaism means to teach not just facts, but values and traditions, and moreover, commitment to those values and traditions. (self-evaluation, September 1995)

Her commitment was palpable. A clinical supervisor who observed her during the semester noted her strengths: her ability to engage the children, her enthusiasm, and her charisma. After visiting her classroom, he wrote: "This lesson was executed beautifully. Nehama is a wonderful 'actress'; She is a real charmer. Nehama is a *very* talented young woman" (1996; underlining his).

Developing a strong rapport with Rina, her cooperating teacher, Nehama began to rethink her notion of a day school curriculum. Rina taught for half the day and was paid to work on school-wide projects for the rest of the time. Nehama's concept map depicting the world of day schools changed as a result of this association.

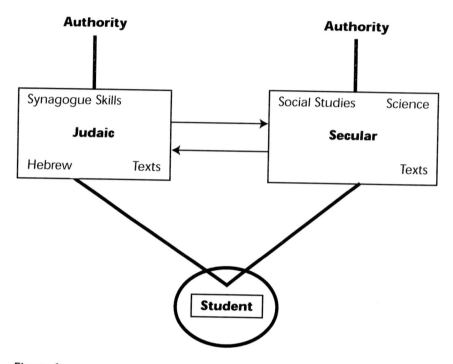

Figure 1

Her concept map of 1994, prior to student teaching, reflects two boxes representing curriculum, one Judaic and one secular; the contents of those boxes are skills and academic subjects. The Judaica box is filled with synagogue skills, Hebrew, and texts; in the secular box, Nehama delineated social studies, science, and texts. This was the curriculum of the school that she had attended, as best as she could recall it. She was still thinking like a student and not a teacher. In her depiction of a day school in 1996, a year and a half later (Figure 2), the rigid curricular boxes have given way to softer circles, still labeled "Judaic" and "secular."

Within those circles, Nehama includes cocurricular learning experiences such as trips, plays, and special projects, as well as "subjects." (Like the school Nehama attended as a child, the school in which she did her student teaching adhered to a divided day, with half the time devoted to Judaic subjects and half the time devoted to general education.)

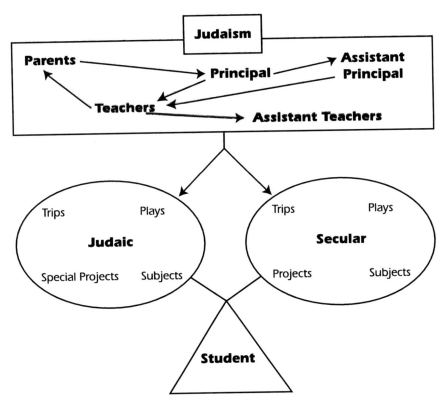

Figure 2

Our exchange about the concept map of 1996 (Figure 2) reflected the influence of Nehama's work with Rina and captured the spirit of our collaboration in the limning of her portrait.

> *Nehama:* [pointing to the circles labeled "Judaic" and "secular"] It's not only strictly academic by the book. The students spend so much time in day schools. They learn so much, and they learn it also through the plays and through trips and whatever else they do during the day.
>
> *CKI:* It's interesting, and now maybe this is just a fluke, and maybe I'm reading too much into this. . . .

Nehama: Because I worked with Rina, who did all the special projects. Maybe because someone else, another teacher who worked full time, whose focus is on his or her students [author's note: rather than the students of the entire school], doesn't have the time or inclination to think about the *zimriyah* [songfest], which I just went to the other night, or a play, or bulletin boards, or things like that, which Rina would spend a signifi-cant amount of time on. She'd spend half her day on it. So half her job was classroom teaching and half of her job was special projects, which I think encompasses school curriculum. *(inter-view, 1996)*

This interview was telling, reinforcing my contention that Nehama un-derstood a basic truth that, according to Campbell (1990–91), experts in teaching acquire over time: teaching is a situation-specific craft. Working with Rina gave Nehama a viewpoint about teaching and life in schools that she might not have acquired had she been placed in another classroom. And she knew this.

After completing her semester of student teaching, Nehama felt con-fident about her professional and personal skills and looked forward to obtaining her first full-time job in a day school. In her self-evaluation, she observed:

I often greeted my students in the mornings with smiles, hugs, and "high fives." While these informal exchanges continued throughout the day and overflowed into my teaching time, it was always clear that I was not only a friendly face, but their teacher as well. After a short adjustment period at the beginning of my [student] teaching experience, my students knew that when I was standing in front of the room, and should be treated as such. *(self-evaluation, 1996)*

But Nehama's confidence as to her ability to relate to her students did not extend to her command of the Hebrew language. That spring, she had a job interview that was conducted in Hebrew, in which she felt that she had performed miserably. Hoping to join a day school with an integrated Judaica and general studies program, Nehama was very dis-appointed when the principal of Morasha Day School offered her a po-sition as an assistant teacher instead of giving her a classroom of her own. But in Nehama's matter-of-fact, accepting style, she decided to make the best of the situation. Like the dancer she was trained to be, she stumbled, but continued on. After all, an assistantship was a foot in the door and an opportunity to grow under supervision.

> I'll be able to try new things, new approaches to classroom management and other areas and have it be safe. I can go to my teacher first and say, "Well, what do you think of this? Is this going to work? Is it okay to teach a lesson this way—to divide them up into groups this way instead of that way?" *(interview, 1996)*

As early as her first full-time professional position, Nehama knew that there was no formula, no one-size-fits-all approach to teaching. Britzman (1991) characterizes prospective teachers as believing in the cultural myth of the "teacher as expert." What counts as expertise is the acquisition of tricks of the trade. When I asked her what she hoped to gain from working with a senior teacher, Nehama readily admitted that she had a lot to learn but was quick to add that she didn't expect to become anyone's clone.

> Classroom management, behavior management: these are areas that I simply don't know as much about. I'll be able to watch my teacher and see how she does it. I'll be able to model that, I hope, *with my own flair. (interview, 1996; italics mine)*

While Britzman's teachers could not imagine "the specificity of the pedagogical act" (1991, p. 227), Nehama could. She hoped that the year would provide her with what she called the "insight" of the expert teacher who could adapt curriculum to students and to work that adaptation around her strengths as a teacher.

CKI: Insight into what?

Nehama: Oh, the students, the age of the students, knowing what an individual student is going to need or what an individual student can give. Insight into what kinds of lessons will work on a given day. To be even more specific, on a rainy day. Maybe they need to be doing other things, running around or something like that. I think things like that come with experience that I certainly don't have. *(interview, 1996)*

In addition, Nehama did not subscribe to Britzman's third cultural myth: that teachers are self-made—that teaching is a gift that one either has or does not have (1991). Although disappointed in the job that she was offered, Nehama was determined to treat her position as an extension of her graduate school experience, an opportunity to continue to grow by experimenting with a new curriculum, new methodologies, acquiring some fancy footwork by watching a seasoned professional, while finding her distinctive style. (This approach, extending preservice education to cover the first year of teaching, has been implemented by Israel's Department of Education since 2002 for all teachers hoping to become certified.)

Early Years of Teaching: Joining the Corps de Ballet

It was May, and Nehama's first year of teaching, albeit as an assistant teacher, was coming to an end. We had barely begun our annual interview, when Nehama described the tension that she had been experiencing all year.

> *Nehama:* The English [author's note: general studies] teacher is a new teacher. This isn't her first time in a classroom; she has been an assistant for a couple of years. She has had other classroom experiences, but this is her first time as the responsible one. In addition, she has trouble asking for help, so if there is a lesson in which she needs help, she won't ask me. She'll expect me to know what's going to happen and then gets angry with me when I don't know.
>
> *CKI:* It sounds like a marriage when . . .
>
> *Nehama:* It is exactly how they describe a marriage . . .
>
> *CKI:* . . . one of the partners doesn't say, "This is what I need."
>
> *Nehama:* Right. On another note, the general communication [between the two teachers] in the classroom has been miserable, and, therefore, that element of my job has been close to miserable. *(interview, 1997)*

According to Nehama, the Judaic studies teacher, a veteran of twenty years, missed her former co-teacher of two years, someone with whom she was professionally and personally very comfortable. The relationship between this veteran and a relatively new teacher with whom she was expected to partner had become so strained that, according to Nehama, the Judaica specialist "was ready to quit." Like Suzy, Nehama was disappointed in the people with whom she had to work closest. But in her determinedly upbeat way, Nehama shifted gears and began to retreat from the glum picture that she had just painted.

> Despite the fact that it didn't work out, I really enjoyed having two other people to work with. Certainly, it hasn't been miserable every minute, but at the same time I feel like I've spent so much more time and energy worrying about the relationship and less time worrying about the children. *(interview, 1997)*

Nehama's hopes of picking up more pedagogical content knowledge were realized, despite the tension between the two teachers. The Judaica specialist taught her several techniques to infuse the class with more Hebrew, such as repeating student questions—as if the teacher didn't understand—in Hebrew that were asked in English, using Hebrew captions on the bulletin boards, and introducing new vocabulary with accompanying pictures. What came as the greatest surprise to Nehama was how much she enjoyed teaching reading with the general studies specialist, something she resented when she first learned that it was part of her job description. She admitted that despite her determination to be cheerful about it, she was annoyed that she was hired as a lowly assistant teacher.

> *Nehama:* I walked into reading group with an even bigger chip on my shoulder: "I don't belong here. This is not what I teach. This is not what I'm trained to teach," which was a destructive attitude, I think, looking back.
>
> *CKI:* Reading group meaning reading group in English?
>
> *Nehama:* English reading group. Yes.
>
> *CKI:* And you were thinking, "Boy, I've got a degree in. . . ."
>
> *Nehama:* "Judaic studies. I don't know anything about this. . . . I don't want to be here." It was a destructive attitude, for a few reasons. First of all, that was my job, and I needed to suck it up . . .
>
> *CKI:* [laughing] Is that the technical language, "suck it up"?

Nehama: [laughing] Absolutely. You can quote me on that.
(interview, 1997)

In describing their methodology, Lawrence-Lightfoot and Davis maintain that the portraitist must begin with an attitude that appreciates goodness, not one that idealizes the subject of the portrait, but is one of "acceptance and discernment, generosity and challenge" (1997, p. 141). Nehama's retelling of her difficulties with the secular studies teacher and her reluctance to embrace her assignment highlight her personal strengths of reflection and flexibility.

> *Nehama:* The general studies teacher with whom I work clearly noticed my attitude and was then reluctant to give me any kind of responsibility whatsoever. And then we got into a groove of not giving me responsibility, which has continued.
>
> *CKI:* And were you resentful of not being given responsibility?
>
> *Nehama:* No.
>
> *CKI:* No? You just continued to say, "That's not my job"?
>
> *Nehama:* [nodding] And then as I continued to work, I became interested in what I was seeing, once I let myself. I ended up taking a class at Livingston College in teaching reading. [author's note: Nehama paid for the class herself.] I really grew because of it. I saw the value in it, and then when I took the class, saw connections between it and what I did want to teach. So it really was good that way. *(interview, 1997)*

Nehama's qualities of unflagging buoyancy and dogged optimism, her ability to recognize her own errors and to grow even in less than optimal situations, were a constant throughout her interviews. She had hoped to pay her dues, spend a year being an assistant teacher, and then work her way into her own classroom. This didn't happen; in telling me about this, Nehama muses, "Man plans, and God laughs" *(interview, 1998)*. Because of no teacher openings and the vagaries of her husband's schedule, she was once again offered an assistant teacher position, working with the same team. I registered some surprise that the administration hadn't moved the players around, given what Nehama had said about the unpleasantness of their personal and professional interactions over the year. She said:

Yeah. With the same team. I think the second year is always better than the first year. It will be the second year for the general studies teacher. She'll know the curriculum, so she'll be less stressed. When she's stressed, she wears it on her sleeve and has a lot of trouble doing anything else but being stressed. I hope that between now and the beginning of September, we'll sit down and talk about this year and how to make next year better. And there are ways. I think the Judaic studies teacher entered this relationship with the knowledge that her partner for the past two years was (a) super and (b) one who did things in one particular way. I think this Judaic studies teacher entered this year assuming that things would be the same—that this general studies teacher would assume the same responsibilities as the other one, and everything would be great. But it didn't happen that way because they're different people. So I think we'll go into it with our eyes open, and it's got to be better. It can't be worse. *(interview, 1997)*

It did, in fact, become worse. The three teachers never did sit down and have that conversation about the past year and how to build a team for the coming year. No one took the initiative, and the administration never did intervene. Nehama kept hoping that the situation would improve. Offered a pay raise to sweeten the offer of yet another year as an assistant teacher, Nehama was pragmatic. "I thought, 'Well, okay. I'm getting more money for doing the same thing that I did last year' " *(interview, 1998)*.

Nehama became pregnant and left the faculty in February. She chatted with me in June as she held her three-month-old son.

Nehama: And this is how life worked out. Here we are moving to Westwood.

CKI: Well, I'm looking at what you're bouncing on your hip, and that's certainly a good resolution. Not that you planned it that way. . . .

Nehama: Right, but it got me out.

CKI: That's interesting language—"It got me out." It sounds like you really wanted . . .

Nehama: I was sick. I was sick of that situation. I didn't much enjoy working with those people. It wasn't a fun place to go.

The kids, though, were terrific—absolutely wonderful. *(interview, 1998)*

Nehama's description of a dysfunctional team-teaching situation is hardly a rarity in the literature. The promise of team teaching is one of cooperation, pooling talents, exposing children to diversity in subject-matter expertise, pedagogy, and personalities. For a team to succeed, there must be an atmosphere of sharing and professionalism, where good communication is the norm. Schamber (1999) describes the goal:

> The establishment of this atmosphere requires a concerted effort on the part of all team members. Past differences need to be forgiven and forgotten, personality differences need to be set aside as much as humanly possible, experienced teachers need to be receptive to the ideas of less experienced teachers who may have the knowledge of recent research on best practice, and new teachers need to respect the voice of experience. (p. 23)

When members of the team cannot create this atmosphere, someone else must serve as mediator, moving the team through the five stages that Buckley recommends: exodus (seeing another's viewpoint), revelation (attentive listening), empathy, goal-setting, and covenant (establishing a plan for working together) (2000, pp. 61–62). Without an intervention, the team self-destructs, as Nehama's experience testifies.

Moving to a New Studio: Teaching in a Synagogue School

The arrival of a new baby and an unpleasant experience during her year and a half of teaching in a day school were reasons enough to leave day school teaching for the short term. (In his study of CAJE members, Schaap [2002] notes that 11.3% left for family reasons [p. 15].) But as Nehama's son grew older, she began to feel isolated and eager to work part-time. During the summer of 1998, Nehama decided to teach a few hours a week in a synagogue school in Elmwood, a suburb close to her home in Westwood. The fact that the school was led by a principal who used to be a fellow graduate student was an incentive, as was the part-time nature of the position, the additional income, and the opportunity to polish her teaching skills. Nehama taught there for three years, from 1998 until 2001. I asked her what she learned from this less intensive experience of teaching in a synagogue school as opposed to a day school, and she replied:

> Especially in Hebrew school—which is what I know now, which may be different from day school, but in some ways not—the [quality of the educational experience that the students receive] is maybe more important than what they learn sometimes. Not to negate the importance of the content, but that they come out of Hebrew school happy is what's going to make them want to come back, not that they know every single word of *Mah Nish-tanah*. And once they continue to come back and are happy, then you can push the words of *Mah Nishtanah*. But first they have to want to be there, and if they're bored by learning the *Sh'ma* for that day, you stop doing it, and you sing a song, or you play charades, or you do something else that's going to make their day happier at that place. *(interview, 2000)*

Nehama's resilience and her grasp of children and classroom life had given her a set of pedagogic strategies that resemble those of expert teachers (Campbell, 1990–91). As important as her commitment to cultural literacy was in her early professional development ("My subject is Judaism. To teach Judaism means to teach not just facts, but values and traditions, and moreover, commitment to those values and traditions" [September 1995]), Nehama had learned to retreat in order to advance. She mused, "I don't think that a person would change as much if they *know* the *aleph-bet* backward and forward as they would if they *enjoyed* learning the *aleph-bet* backward and forward" *(interview, 2000)*.

I asked Nehama if she thought that her insights about the affective aspect of Jewish education apply to day school teaching as well as teaching in a synagogue school. She observed that synagogue schools paradoxically have an edge over day schools. Not being considered "real school" allows for more freedom vis-à-vis synagogue schools.

Nehama: [The pressure to achieve more is offset by] more time to develop relationships between the kids, between the teacher and the kids, between the school to have other celebrations and school-wide programs and art and music, and things we don't have in Hebrew school. So yes, I feel like the nature of the beast lends itself heavier to the content area, but I think also the nature of the beast is that it's more of it, and it's sort of . . . I can't think of the word . . . where it just seeps into you because you're there all the time.

CKI: Osmosis?

Nehama: Yeah, that's the word. If you're there for nine years all day long, there's a better chance that it's just going to become a part of you than if you're there for seven hours a week. *(interview, 2000)*

After two years of undergraduate teaching, two years of graduate education, a year and a half of day school teaching, and three years of teaching in a synagogue school, Nehama was beginning to feel that she had found her footing as a teacher. She mulled over how novice teachers differ from experts.

Nehama: In the beginning I was terrified, or a novice is terrified. I'll never forget the first time I walked into a classroom and someone had to say, "Nehama, don't forget that you're twice as old as these students." (I was twenty; they were ten.) And I *had* forgotten that; they were going to take over as far as I was concerned.

CKI: When you say take over, you're talking about discipline?

Nehama: I mean there are fifteen of them and one of me. Yeah.

CKI: There are just more of them?

Nehama: There are just more of them, and they're smarter than I am, and they're cooler than I am, and they know what it's like to be ten, and I don't any more. You know, just that general fear of walking in. . . . Not that I'm not nervous every September because I am, like every teacher is, forever. I hope so. I mean just not being as terrified. . . .

CKI: Why do you think that it would be dreadful if teachers weren't nervous? You said that you hope that they'll always be nervous. Why?

Nehama: Because then they just become lazy and not challenged. I think of the day school experience that I now live through my husband. He tells me that the teachers who have been there for twenty or twenty-five years are bitter. All they want is their days off. They don't want to do anything extra other than what's in their classroom, whereas Sam [Nehama's husband], who's a brand-new teacher, will do anything and everything and always volunteers and doesn't understand why the twenty-year veterans aren't like that. *(interview, 2000)*

I asked Nehama when she felt most like a real teacher. She recalled a family education program she prepared for Hanukkah, describing the parents as initially coming out of a sense of duty, not expecting much more than the usual craft project.

Nehama: I did a family workshop for the Aleph class, which is what I teach in Hebrew school. It was a new program. I made it up, a little from here, a little from there. I called it "The Search for God in Elmwood," which is where the school is. You look in the siddur. Where do you find God there? And you look in a mirror. Where do you find God there? And you look at the names of God. What are your favorite ones and why?

CKI: You look in a real mirror?

Nehama: Yes and there were actual mirrors. Look in them. What do you see? Where do you see God? What's special about you? What's special about your mom? How is that God or not God? I know that these parents walked in thinking that they were going to walk out with a *hanukkiyah* that they made. I'm sure that that's what they were thinking. They were going to sing some songs, and they were gonna play *dreidel.* And they walked out having discussed God. They were so impressed, and I got terrific feedback. They thought that they'd be doing those other things because that's what every other teacher had done in all their years with their other children. I was different, and that was good. I challenged them. *(interview, 2000)*

Since her student-teaching days in graduate school, Nehama had been expanding her definition of curriculum. The professional example of which she was so proud was one that included an expanded curriculum, one big enough to encompass discussions of God, spirituality, and personal meaning-making, something absent in the conventional curriculum for her class. Not only did she delight in God-talk with her students but also with the parents of the students she taught.

But Nehama was ambivalent about the synagogue school. While discussing her teaching over the past several years, Nehama repeatedly used phrases such as, "It's not real school. It's not that full day, full week, year-round experience" *(interview, 2000)*. Jewish day school was the real thing.

Yet Nehama was not naïve about the second-class status of Jewish learning in liberal day schools. When I probed, she readily admitted that in day schools, Judaica subjects were not afforded the same respect as their general studies counterparts:

> Various teachers in Sam's school have a rehearsal [for a play], so the students are pulled out of *Humash* class. They're not pulled out of math. You know, the year's coming to an end and they have to practice for graduation, so they're pulled out of *Humash* class, or *Navi*, or Hebrew. *Humash* is three times a week whereas language arts is four or five. So it's definitely second even when it's supposed to be the same. *(interview, 2000)*

Nehama worried about the corrosive influence of contemporary American culture, a landscape strewn with enormous obstacles for any teacher of religious education or anyone who wants to send a counter-cultural, transgressive message. Like Suzy, she saw herself as a moral educator, not just as an information jockey:

> You know the sex, drugs, and rock and roll; the guns. I think moral education is not what this society is teaching us. That is, the core of religious education is to be a good person in whatever framework you choose or were born into, and to achieve a higher standard. I think the sex, drugs, and rock and roll of society, which I guess have always been there, challenge that in a lot of ways. Is it more so now? Maybe. I feel like I'm fifty years old. Maybe on the computer, there's more stuff and it's more accessible. And the music these kids listen to is terrible, but that's just me. But my parents said that, too, so I don't know whether

the '90s posed different problems from those of the '80s, '70s, or '60s or if it's the same. *(interview, 2000)*

But knowing what was out there was crucial to Nehama's pedagogy. She had learned that education takes place in a context and that successful teaching must respond to students' needs. She defined her task as "understanding the greater society that the child lives in and what the material I'm dealing with is. And I have to mold this person based on all these other outside things" *(interview, 2000)*.

"Dancing: The Highest Intelligence in the Freest Body" (Isadora Duncan)

Qualitative research uses a different set of criteria to ascertain validity than does quantitative research. The researcher must look for areas of agreement, in interviews over time, and in various data sources. Using concept maps afforded me another data source, another vehicle to help me re-create Nehama's views about teaching in a Jewish day school. Nehama's concept maps, like her interviews, changed significantly over time. They corroborated the impression that one receives from the transcripts of our conversations—that Nehama's thinking had become freer, more inclusive, and more nuanced.

I have referred earlier to Nehama's changing notions of curriculum. "This is based on my experience as a student," she began *(interview, 1994)*, and then she depicted learning to be bounded and fixed (Figure 1). Jewish knowledge and general studies coexist in separate domains ("I put all the content in boxes"). Students are passive vessels waiting to be filled with finite knowledge, packaged as Jewish studies and general studies:

> When I think of Centerville [Nehama's alma mater], Jewish studies and general studies are very separate. There are the Judaic studies, the secular studies, and never the two shall meet. And their goal is what? Their goal is probably to create one person that has both equally, so if the student is down here [pointing to the bottom of the page]—maybe it should have been a circle, so it's a well-rounded student—that's what they're trying to create. *(interview, 1994)*

Knowledge in this kind of school was handed down by authorities, the subject specialists, who packed learning into discrete boxes labeled "Judaic" and "secular." What Michael Apple (1990) might call "high status" Jewish learning included synagogue skills, Hebrew, and texts. Their corollary, "high status" secular learning, encompassed social studies, science, and texts. Teachers served as funnels, somehow softening the sharp edges of their squared students, turning them into fully integrated people who could be comfortable in both the secular and Judaic realms. This concept map shares a great deal with that of Suzy, drawn at the same time. It is a school seen through a student's eyes, with the myopia of a student.

After the completion of student teaching (Figure 2), Nehama broadened her definition of curriculum, including the school-wide, cocurricular activities that were the domain of her cooperating teacher and mentor. Trips, plays, and special projects appear in her drawing. She no longer defined the Judaic and secular curricula by the neat subject-centered categories. The life of schools flows over the classroom walls; it is more than academic subjects in neat, separate packages. She had developed a more peripheral vision.

Nehama was ambivalent about integration, a much commonly touted, and usually ill-defined, term in the world of Jewish day schools.* Poised to graduate and take a first job in a day school, she found integration an appealing concept, one that played a minor role in her own schooling. I asked her if the school in which she student taught supported integration.

Nehama: I think that the school doesn't purposely integrate, but by the fact that it goes into the same brain that it ultimately in some way . . . it becomes integrated.

CKI: So the student is doing the integrating?

Nehama: Right. I think inevitably it's that because it goes like this [tracing the line on her concept map] into the brain, and then maybe later in life that student figures out how it all goes together . . . or not. I don't know.

---

*For a fuller treatment of the issue of integration, see M. Malkus, "Portraits of Curricular Integration in Jewish Day Schools," Ph.D. diss., Jewish Theological Seminary, 2001.

CKI: You're saying that maybe day schools shouldn't be doing the integration and that the student has to struggle with making sense and meaning out of this? It's not the job of the school to create that synthesis.

Nehama: I don't know what I'm saying. That's the ideal. I think the ideal would be more synthesis. Second-graders don't know how to integrate the material necessarily. They internalize it. They learn it. It all goes to the same brain, but at the same time I think it would be better in several areas to combine [Jewish and general studies]. Maybe they would have a deeper understanding of the two issues—the secular and the Judaic issue—if they were viewed as together if they were presented as being integrated. I don't know that my education was integrated, but I don't think I'm any worse for the wear. I think, though, that when I see integration it gets me excited. It's great, super. I see a different view of the materials as they are together, and I think, "Wow, isn't that great! That's what we do here in America—we integrate." So I drew the picture because that's how it is. It's not terrible the way it is; it's worked fine. I think it could work a little better if it were a little more integrated. *(interview, 1996)*

Nehama's insight—that for all its appeal, integration by design, whether it is content integration or skills integration, may not always be necessary—is one shared by no less an educational luminary than Israel Scheffler. In reflecting upon his own day school education, Scheffler comments:

[T]he curriculum itself comprised two worlds, that of traditional Jewish culture and experience, and that of "general," non-Jewish, culture and experience. These worlds presented multiple oppositions—between the religious and the secular, the old and the new, the heritage of our people and the heritage of others, the loyalties due our past and the challenge of our future, the ideals of community and the ideology of individualism, Jewish belonging and life in a multi-national America. The school said nothing about these oppositions, offered no reconciliations or philosophical rationalizations. It simply incorporated these two worlds within itself and, by offering them both to us as our daily fare, it built them both into our consciousness, bequeathing to us at the same time the ragged boundaries and the gnawing conflicts between them. (1995, p. 86)

Nehama's concept maps become more and more farsighted, documenting a growing awareness of the stakeholders in the educational enterprise. Her first diagram (Figure 1), drawn after one semester of graduate school, portrays the world of day school education as an enterprise that includes educators and students only. Parents are nonexistent. However, parents appear on each of her subsequent drawings. Nehama's discussion of the world of day schools was marked by her understanding of the multiple roles that parents can play in the schooling of their children. Having seen parents interact with Rina and other teachers in her student-teaching placement (Figure 2), Nehama realized, long before her peers, that parents, as advocates for their children, shaped the curriculum through their relationships with teachers and administrators. In her drawing, parents are on the same plane as the educators in the school; they, along with their fellow interpreters of Judaism, the principal, assistant principal, teachers, and assistant teachers, serve as agents of socialization and transmitters of cultural literacy (see Figure 2). Nehama also replaced the subject specialist "authorities" with Judaism as the driving force in her depiction. The day school answers to a higher authority, in the words of the Hebrew National ad. That authority isn't the superintendent or those who determine what will be on the Regents' exam; it is Judaism.

By the end of her first year of teaching, Nehama was grappling with parents as clients keenly interested in the well-being of their children, clients who expect value for what they buy. Like Suzy, Nehama had learned that a day school exists in a market economy.

At the center of the paper, I placed the child [pointing to the concentric circles at the top of the diagram] because that is still the focus of this whole thing, the reason the day school exists. I put a circle around it to signify the parents, because the parents protect the child and have the child's best interests in mind at all times. Whether it is, in fact, the child's best interests, that's [another question]. . . . They're protecting their child. I put a dollar sign in there because that's really one of the driving forces of a day school. Whether [or not] you take care of the people who give a lot of money, you're nice to those people, or we have this program because we have money, or we don't have this pro-

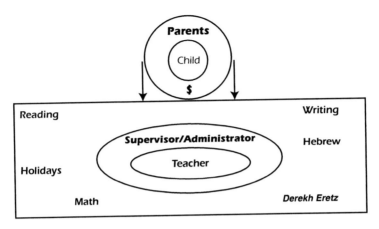

Figure 3

gram because we don't have the money—so that's really a crucial issue. *(interview, 1997)*

Nehama's fourth concept map (Figure 4) was drawn after she completed her first year of teaching. In this drawing, the parents have
moved to the center, being influenced by and influencing all the other
stakeholders (e.g., the director/principal, teachers, specialists, and children). Nehama included the lay leadership of the school: the board
(twice!), the fund-raising arm of the school, and the lay committees.

In her third drawing, teachers are protected by supervisors and administrators (Figure 3). In contrast, the fourth drawing (Figure 4) depicts the teachers off to the side, influencing and influenced by parents.
They are but one element in a complicated lay and professional structure. In interpreting her drawing, Nehama explicated for me the role of
parents and her growing understanding of the school, no longer as the
place where transfer of information occurs but as a complex organizational entity with parents in the center:

> The parents are in the middle in that they make it happen for their
> child. I don't know how to put it: it's everything they do for their
> child. At the same time, it's the parents who give back and make
> things happen, such as the board, the committees, the fund-raising.
> The school wouldn't happen without the parents. I'm looking at
> this now and seeing that this [drawing] is more from a structural

point of view as opposed to an educational point of view. I mean, I didn't put down general studies, Judaic studies. *(interview, 1998)*

  Gone is the driving force of the subject specialists depicted in her first concept map and the authority of Judaism in the second. The engine of day school life changes subtly between her third drawing and her fourth. In the third (Figure 3), Nehama depicted the powerful nexus of parents and children, fueled by the power of money. In the fourth (Figure 4), Nehama placed the parents front and center, the children just one factor, along with the teachers, in the life of the school. Any reference to the curriculum had disappeared. Lay leaders, alluded to in the two board references, the committees, and fund-raising, assume great prominence. Nehama's third and fourth concept maps displayed her growing understanding of what Deborah Ball (1987) calls the "micropolitics" of schools. Nehama's voice gathered speed as she thought about her drawings, her second year of teaching, and her discovery:

  It's true—nothing can happen without the parents. Everything happens with the parents in mind. Yes, and the child. You know, even when you speak to a child, you're thinking, "How is that child going to respond?" But always in the back of your mind is, "What is that child going to tell their parents?" *(interview, 1998)*

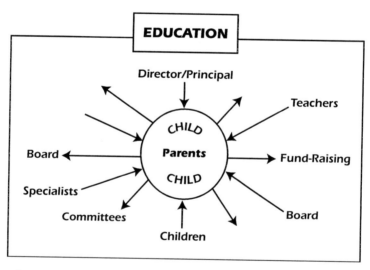

Figure 4

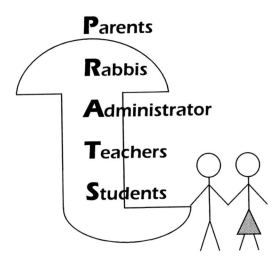

Figure 5

After watching Nehama cuddle her three-month old as we spoke, I tentatively asked her if her professional views had been shaped by her personal situation: Did becoming a mother boost the prominence of parents in her view of schooling? She laughed and responded, "I'll bet you're right" *(interview, 1998)*.

In her last drawing (Figure 5), completed after teaching in a synagogue school as well as a day school, four years after receiving a master's degree in Jewish education, and watching her husband, Sam, negotiate the world of day school teaching, Nehama created a drawing that appeared at first to be simpler, yet in fact was more complex and even more grounded in the reality of schools.

Nehama drew two stick figures, one male, one female, holding an umbrella with the letter "P" over it. The "P" stands for parents. The umbrella is labeled "R" for rabbi, "A" for her principal of the Elmwood Jewish Center, "T" for teachers, and "S" for students. Nehama's explicit acknowledgment of the reciprocal nature of the relationships. When I ask Nehama whom the stick figures were meant to represent, she responds in her typically pragmatic manner, reflecting the reality of a seasoned teacher:

> I think in any institution, but especially in a school, you need to become very close and quick friends with the maintenance man and the person who's going to make your photocopies—who's

going to really support the school in that way. They call them support staff for a reason. I think they hold this umbrella up and make it possible for it all to happen. *(interview, 2000)*

Lawrence-Lightfoot and Davis (1997) describe portraiture as a joint enterprise between the portraitist and the subject of the portrait, a collaboration that unites two visions and blends two voices. It is Nehama who noticed that the umbrella shape in her most recent concept map (Figure 5) appears in rudimentary form in earlier concept maps. In 1996 (Figure 2), it is a semicircle labeled "Judaism"; in 1997 (Figure 3), there are a set of concentric circles perched atop the curriculum like lions on a Torah ark as parents protecting their children (sometimes with the power of the pocketbook).

I asked Nehama to explore this emergent theme of protection. Parents, Judaism, and the support staff of schools all protect. If the umbrella in her fifth concept map symbolized protection, then what was the rain? Her response epitomized her matter-of-fact, hardheaded perception of the realities of school life.

Nehama: The parents protect the school from financial failure, which is for some reason the first thing that comes to mind. 'Cause most of the committees are fund-raising committees, and that's what they do, that's how the place functions. They protect their children from, or they insure [*sic*] that their children are learning what they feel is right, so they're protecting them from things they don't want them to learn, I guess.

CKI: Sex, drugs, and rock and roll, for example?

Nehama: Right, right. *(interview, 2000)*

In June 2001, Nehama left her position at Elmwood for a number of reasons. She now had two children instead of one, her friend had resigned her position as principal, and there were changes in the teaching staff. Nehama was ready to leave the religious school and the field of Jewish education. She told me that she thought she would come back to day school teaching when her children were older and ready to attend day school as students. She knew of Shoshana, a woman older than she, who entered day school teaching when her youngest was ready for kindergarten. Nehama had a long view. If Shoshana could wait for twelve years, so could she. For the time being, Nehama wanted to nurture her own children, not those of others.

Epilogue

I kept up with Nehama's growing family over the years. In 2000, days after our last formal interview, she gave birth to her second child, Ariella—who was a handful, as described by her mother. Ariella, now four, had a big brother, Noam, currently enrolled in a day school. It was Nehama's pregnancy with Noam that had given her the excuse to leave her position at the Morasha Day School. In addition, there was a newcomer to the family: Daniella, Nehama's third child, an easy two-year-old. I spoke to Nehama in June 2004, after the kids were in bed and after her first day on the job as a teacher in a Jewish day camp. She told me that she was thrilled to be getting back to Jewish education, having just begun to work outside of the home for the first time since Ariella's birth four years earlier.

Nehama: This past year I've been doing *Minyan Katan* twice a month for my synagogue. It's a prayer experience for kids under six.

CKI: You've got three little kids. Why did you go back to work?

Nehama: Why do you ever do things? If I didn't do it, no one would do it. I did it for my kids and to keep my foot in the door, to keep my brain functioning. I love it. My kids all went. Now I'm working as a teacher in a day camp, with the five-to-eight-year-olds. The first session, there's an Israel-based curriculum: cities, then food, then a sort of "One People, Many Faces" curriculum. There's a Torah curriculum for the second session.

CKI: Did you have to design the curriculum?

Nehama: They gave us a notebook with lesson plans, but there are still holes for us to fill. Today was the first day. I loved it. It was great getting my feet wet again, getting my brain functioning. I plan to go back to *Minyan Katan* in the fall. I'm doing something I love to do. Little kids are my niche. I'm good at it. Interacting, going with the flow. They're not threatening. I'm always afraid that the older kids are smarter than I am.

It is impossible to miss the robustness of Nehama's implicit theories. She is centered in her role of parent and, as with so many teachers, finds her parenting inextricably connected to career. Nehama teaches a children's service in order to be a better parent; as a young teacher, she has always understood the role of parents in school life far better than her single or newly married peers do. As Sikes (1997) notes, being a parent affects one's teaching, and being a teacher affects one's parenting. Nehama also repeats what she has said earlier: curricula are not carved in stone. They are always adaptable to the context. No matter how polished, they all have "holes"; the holes are filled when a teacher calls on her personal, professional knowledge of who her students are and who she, the teacher, is. I also noted a third recurring theme, and I reminded Nehama of it: she was still a little fearful of her students and needed reassurance that she could handle ten-year-olds.

> *Nehama:* [laughing] I remember that [fear]. I even remember who the friend [who reassured me] was. I've already told Sam [Nehama's husband] that, when my kids are that age, I'm outta here. It'll be fine. [When they're ten,] they're middle-school age—and he's good with them. [Sam taught middle school.] These little kids put me in a good mood.

Nehama recapped her day school teaching experience for me and told me why she left:

> I always said that Morasha was a great place to be a kid but a hard place to be a teacher. The kids had attention [from the professional staff], resources, and teachers to help them. But it was hard work and a lot of pressure to be a teacher there. The parents were always there. Maybe in the fifth grade it was different, but in the second grade the parents were always there. The teachers would stay till dinnertime or late at night. It shouldn't be [that way]. I had a short experience, only two years: I learned some, but not a lot. Overall, I'd say it was positive but challenging.

Parents can raise funds to provide much-needed resources for teachers, easing one's life as a teacher, but parents can be intrusive and demanding. Parents can be two-edged swords, as Nehama, a teacher and parent, describes them.

CKI: Would you elaborate? What do you mean by "challenging" or "hard"? You mentioned the hard work and the late hours.

Nehama: The team teaching. There were teachers with different worldviews, different personalities, coming from different cultures.

CKI: Is there any way to do a better job with setting up the teams?

Nehama: What made it hard was mostly about personality. Sometimes different personalities make for a healthy team. How can you know who's going to match before you match them? It's the luck of the draw.

CKI: Could there have been an intervention?

Nehama: You mean therapy? [laughs] There was no one available to do it, and the people need to want to change. The attitude was, "Let's just get this job done." There was so much pressure because of so little time.

CKI: What else made it hard?

Nehama: The newness of it, I suppose. Then, too, I wasn't in charge. It wasn't my class; it wasn't my job to make decisions.

This issue of autonomy is crucial in describing the life of a professional (Aron, 1990). It is an echo of Suzy's disappointment in her administration second-guessing her professionalism. For all her good humor and her desire to be a good team player, Nehama wanted a class to call her own.

CKI: Usually, not making decisions is comforting for a novice.

Nehama: I needed to make peace. I felt as if I held it all together. I was torn between feeling I needed to fix it and needing to get away.

Like Suzy, Nehama felt spent. The only apparent solution was to leave. I asked her if she could imagine herself going back to day school teaching. This was her plan when we had spoken at length before Ariella's birth in 2000. Nehama replied, "Maybe one day. All my kids would need to be in school. I'd reevaluate when the kids are there. I think I'd really like to teach in an early childhood setting, either in a day school or elsewhere." Having established that being a parent affects one's views of education, I asked Nehama if being the wife of a teacher shaped her views of day school education.

> *Nehama:* Sam is so passionate about it. A lot is innate, who you are. He was a teacher without taking any courses.
>
> *CKI:* But he has taken so many courses. He has a degree, in fact, in special ed.
>
> *Nehama:* That's true. The degree and courses informed him, but he was always a teacher. I learned from doing it, and maybe the period was too short—only two years. Now the thought of going back makes me even more nervous. Classroom management, handling transitions—there are so many tricks to learn, and I didn't learn them.
>
> *CKI:* Do you feel you were still a novice when you left?
>
> *Nehama:* Absolutely. I think the school [JTS] is doing a much better job now. I talk to students in the Davidson School who are working at camp. I tell them that I was there before it was the Davidson School; it was just a part of the graduate school. Now there are so many new courses, such as how to teach Bible. The student teaching experience is longer. I hear that there's going to be an Israel trip for the students. [A wistful looks comes over her.] They're getting much better preparation than I had.

Nehama sees herself as a novice who left the world of day schools before she could claim the expertise that she as a parent would no doubt demand of her children's teachers. She recognizes that even with better preservice education, a later cohort of day school teachers would still have to learn on the job and would still need administrative support to succeed. I think Nehama shortchanges herself. She certainly had begun to think more like a seasoned professional in many areas: in her understanding of the situated nature of learning, in recognizing the complexity of school life, in knowing that no teacher can simply thaw and serve up a curriculum. Whether Nehama returns to day school teaching to continue her evolution to expert status is anyone's guess.

CHAPTER FOUR
Lynn: Sink or Swim

What struck me first about Lynn was how intense she was. She spoke about her desire to become a Jewish educator with such passion. Her brow furrowed, and her voice shook when she became excited. What was most exciting about beginning her graduate studies in Jewish education was the opportunity to engage with Jewish texts. The essay she wrote as part of her application to the education program at the Jewish Theological Seminary documents both her love of Jewish learning and her desire to turn that learning into Jewish living:

> I want to study at JTS first for me and for my own personal knowledge. I have always had a desire to learn more Bible, Talmud, and Hebrew. I want to know more about the hows and whys of Judaism, and the Conservative views in particular on halakhic issues. (admissions essay, February 7, 1994)

In that essay, Lynn describes the thrill of meeting a great Jewish scholar, Simon Greenberg. In traditional circles, the appropriate response is to quietly recite the blessing "Praised are You, Lord our God, King of the universe, who has shared of God's wisdom with those who revere God." Lynn's response, recalled two years later, evoked a reaction like a star sighting, like catching a glimpse of a rock musician doing his grocery shopping:

> A friend and I were reading and discussing the different *teshuvot* [rabbinic responsa] on women's participation in services and mitzvot. All of a sudden . . . Simon Greenberg, who edited the book we were reading, was walking in the door. . . . It was so

incredible to meet the author of one of the *teshuvot*. To be in the presence of such a scholar was a powerful feeling. I am eager to study from other well-known, highly respected scholars. (admissions essay, February 7, 1994)

The essay also touches on a theme that reverberated throughout my conversations with Lynn. Although she chose to go to graduate school primarily to increase her own understanding of Judaism and Jewish texts, acquiring a master's degree in Jewish studies would enable her to pass her love of learning on to others. "Becoming a Jewish educator will give me a chance to channel and direct my passion for Jewish learning. It enables me to give something tangible and lasting back to the community" (admissions essay, February 7, 1994). I found a Sylvia Barrett-in-the-making, a prospective teacher whose proving ground would be a Jewish day school rather than the multicultural, multi-ethnic, multiracial Calvin Coolidge High School.

Lynn was thin and wiry, with long brown hair that rested on her shoulders. She looked bookish, reserved, and serious. Her emotional outbursts came as a surprise. In our initial interview, at the close of her first semester of graduate school, she became outraged as she remembered an event from her childhood. At that time, her father, a day school lay leader, had tried to sell her small Midwestern Jewish community on extending their Jewish day school beyond the sixth grade. He had raised enough funds to enable Lynn's classmates to continue their Jewish education tuition-free. According to Lynn, the prospective students were willing, but their parents wanted a public school experience for their children, "to meet more people." Ten years later, Lynn was still furious. Her voice trembled as she recalled, "I was so angry. I can't tell you how upset I was" *(interview, 1994)*.

Lynn was impatient with those who didn't appreciate Jewish education as she did. They included her classmates' parents who wouldn't take a chance on a new day school, members of the local chapter of USY who were more interested in socializing than in the Jewish content of the programming, and some of her classmates in Sunday school who were less serious than she. "We learned nothing because half the class goofed off. If you wanted to learn anything, forget it." She referred to the synagogue program as "useless," although she rejoined it to participate in a confirmation program *(interview, 1994)*.

The daughter of a general studies teacher in a day school and a lawyer, Lynn is the eldest child in her family. She and her sister and brother grew up in a large extended clan where grandparents, aunts and uncles, and other relatives celebrated Jewish holidays together. Since there were many of her mother's relatives living in her community, there were always cousins in her synagogue, youth group, and classes. She described her Shabbat morning youth service as dominated by her circle of friends and family. "It was mostly me and my cousins, and two or three other families. The ones who were in USY did everything." While Lynn was quick to explain how important family was to her, she was also quick to describe how eager she was to meet new people at Camp Ramah or international conventions staged by USY. There she could meet some of the more serious teenagers beyond the local chapter, who, like Lynn, went for the infusion of Jewish content, not just the socializing.

Her bat mitzvah afforded Lynn an opportunity to demonstrate her seriousness and her steeliness. In her Conservative synagogue, a bat mitzvah took place on a Friday night. The young woman would recite a haftarah after the recitation of the Kabbalat Shabbat service. Knowing that a haftarah is read only on a Sabbath morning, not on a Friday evening, Lynn dismissed that kind of bat mitzvah as "not counting as a service" *(interview, 1994)*. Committed to authenticity and determined to demonstrate the skills that she had acquired in her day school, she and her cousin confronted the congregational rabbi, making their case for a more substantial ceremony. They asked to lead the daily service, which had become familiar to them through their prayer experiences in school, and to read Torah as well. Lynn proudly recalled the rabbi's concession: "Well, if you have a private service on a weekday where the people in the synagogue who object don't have to know, you can have one" *(interview, 1994)*. Lynn and her cousins all became *b'not mitzvah* on a Monday morning, read Torah, and led the service. "The rabbi didn't do anything but was there to maybe call out page numbers or give us a blessing at the end. That was all he did; *it was ours*" *(interview, 1994)*.

I asked Lynn if she felt a tiny bit cheated as well as vindicated. Did she ever feel that she had a second-class bat mitzvah on a Monday morning without a big splashy party on a Saturday evening, as did the other young women she knew? Lynn very quickly responded:

Not at all. I thought mine was better than theirs. I was doing it all. I was doing what I knew, what I wanted to do. I knew more than they did, and honestly, at that point in time I didn't have many friends who went to afternoon school. Most of my friends were there, and my entire day school class—all twelve of us—came, and some of my non-Jewish friends came from junior high.

The resolve, the intensity, and the commitment to learning and Jewish practice are quintessentially Lynn.

After seven years of day school, Lynn attended a public high school. She and a few of her friends continued their Jewish studies throughout high school, working with a tutor who was hired by a few of the more committed parents who were disappointed in the educational level of the local synagogue school. In addition, Lynn attended the synagogue school, which offered a confirmation program. Upon graduation, Lynn left the state to attend Mount Hermon, a demanding university in the Midwest with a large population of Jewish students. There Lynn majored in history and minored in Jewish/Near Eastern studies, accumulating nearly enough credits to graduate with a double major. She chose to spend her junior year in Israel, where she got a taste of Jewish education through a JESNA (Jewish Educational Services of North America)-sponsored experience. (Suzy and Nehama participated in this program as well, but Lynn discussed it in far more detail.) Enjoying her classes and workshops in Jewish education, Lynn began to consider a career in this field. Remembering her years as a camp counselor, she never anticipated having a problem teaching. "I've been teaching swimming for years. I knew I could teach" *(interview, 1994)*. But her internship in a TALI (*Tigbur Limudei Yahadut,* or enhanced Judaic studies) state school was mind-boggling:

> I could walk into class and kids would be running all over, jumping each other, throwing salt in each other's hair, and there was very little that the teachers had in the way of, "If you do this, your punishment is this. If you do that, you're going to the principal." It was basically to separate them. I could do whatever I wanted to these kids—and it felt very odd to me not to be told how to discipline them or how to do something. A kid's jumping around? Okay, pick him up and stick him in the corner. He stays for five minutes and then he's running around again. I was just in shock, appalled. *(interview, 1994)*

Lynn remembered a day when she went to teach and found half the school population missing: there was a teachers' strike. Thrilled that

Lynn showed up, the principal handed her a class. Lynn took one look at the students and remembered thinking, "I'm like, eek! What do I do?" It was very "trying," a word Lynn used often. By the day's close, Lynn's determination and love of learning nearly overcame her anxiety. "It was kind of neat because at the end of the day, it was great. My Hebrew got so much better" *(interview, 1994).*

Returning to Mount Hermon for her senior year, Lynn began to explore different venues in which Jewish education was practiced. She taught for the first time in a local synagogue school and got a taste of informal Jewish education by organizing *shabbatonim* (weekend retreats) for the local Bureau of Jewish Education. The target audience was children in upper elementary school. None of this was like teaching swimming at camp. It was all too reminiscent of Lynn's internship in the TALI school. Once again, in describing the *shabbatonim,* Lynn chooses the word "trying." Once again, she uses, almost verbatim, the description she gave of her classmates and fellow USYers: "The kids definitely didn't always want to be there" *(interview, 1994).* But as "trying" as the *shabbatonim* were, teaching in the religious school was even worse. "I mean, this seventh-grade class was just—it was *bad.* I even team-taught with the assistant rabbi, and they didn't respect him. It was really sad" *(interview, 1994).*

Surely teaching in a day school would be different. Lynn expected that there she would find more serious students—students who resembled the kind of learner she was. I asked Lynn to compare the two kinds of Jewish education: one at a synagogue school and one at a day school.

Oh, my God, there's a world of difference, I think, from what I went through and what I've seen teaching. The stuff that's generic as far as afternoon schools is that kids don't want to be there. They're tired or whatever. They're not paying attention. It's social hour. In day school, they feel that it's real school. Learning Hebrew is part of learning anything. Learning Hebrew is the same as learning math. It's what you do. It's school. You have to do it. You do it every day. It's a given, whereas for afternoon school, you go until your bar or bat mitzvah and then quit. It's very different. Also you have the students only once or twice a week, which makes continuity and discipline very hard. Last year, I had thirty people in my class, but maybe only fifteen of them showed up every week—and it would be a different fifteen every week! So it was very hard to have one subject to teach for a semester. After a while, we sort of gave up on our curriculum for various reasons. One reason was that, except for a small group, the people didn't come every week. *(interview, 1994)*

In that first interview, Lynn seemed to spend a great deal of time talking about discipline. It dominated her thinking. She thought that she might like to teach younger children "because they're easier to deal with." When teachers didn't have discipline, like the ones she saw in her synagogue school experience, it was like swimmers attempting to swim against the current. It was not only "trying," but exhausting. Not only did "the kids not want to be there," but it affected the teachers as well. It wore them out: "Sometimes you get the feeling that the teachers are kind of sluggish, too; they don't know how to teach, or they don't want to teach." If there was no discipline, teachers couldn't function. Lynn described teaching, using language that evoked an image of a cafeteria worker ladling out portions: "The ideal is to give them a basic under-standing of everything—a little bit of Bible, a little bit of Hebrew, a little bit of holidays." If the students don't stand still, the trays will be messy or even empty. She repeated the image of teacher as transmitter else-where in the interview. "I tend to think you're handed the curriculum and told that you're supposed to teach this and this and this" *(interview, 1994)*. Lynn's image of teaching as transmission resembled that de-scribed in *Pirke Avot* (*Ethics of the Fathers*): "Moses received Torah at Sinai and handed it on to Joshua, Joshua to the elders, and the elders to the prophets. And the prophets handed it on to the men of the great as-sembly" (1:1). There is a finite body of knowledge that is handed down from teacher to disciple. In the process, the learner is passive, a recepta-cle for the lore of the ages. According to Stark (1991) and many others, this is the way that novice teachers think about knowledge. It is a com-modity to be acquired and then passed on (p. 294).

When I first asked Lynn to prepare a concept map of a day school, she asked me if I wanted her to depict the Judaic studies dimension and the general studies, or just the Judaic studies. Her question corroborated the impression I had already received: that Lynn could only imagine the stan-dard dual curriculum that characterizes most day schools. It also indicated that her priority was Judaic studies. Teaching general studies, or integra-tion, held no allure for her. Of the three teachers with whom I worked, Lynn was most wedded to envisioning day schools in terms of the day school that she had attended. It was one of her most robust implicit theo-ries, the personal knowledge she had carried around since childhood.

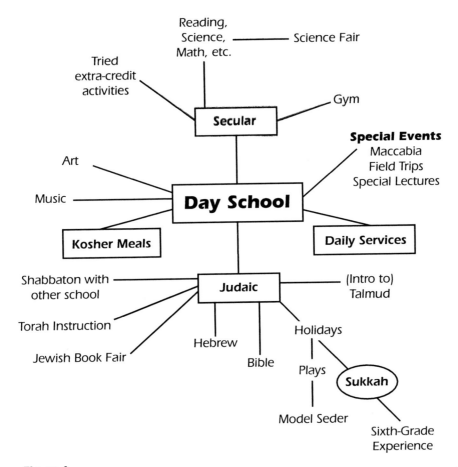

Figure 1

The day school that she had attended was hardly typical; Lynn remembers that a non-Jewish child attended the school, an African American whose parents valued the school for the opportunities that it presented for the study of Bible and Hebrew. Looking over what she had drawn (see Figure 1), Lynn observed, accurately, "My concept of day schools is obviously modeled very much by what I went through" *(interview, 1994)*.

Lynn's first concept map is very concrete and very detailed, full of the nervous energy that is so much a part of her personality. It is a jumble of words. Her concept map is the most detailed and least visual of the three teachers I studied, and the transcriptions of her interviews are the lengthiest. Lynn is a person who is comfortable not only in the world of Jewish texts but in the world of words as well.

She described the school that she had attended: its prayer services, lunch, the dual subjects, and specialties such as art and music, noting as she did that the specialties afforded some of the few opportunities for subject-matter integration. She included sports, field trips, and cocurricular subjects. Her recall was astounding: she remembered a field trip to a farm to cut cornstalks for *sekhakh* (the roof of the sukkah). Lynn's words emerged in a rush, one reminiscence tumbling after another. She slipped into the present tense as she described her 1994 concept map to me:

> There's always a Jewish book fair or other special events, I mean aside from field trips, which could be secular or Judaic-related, or lectures. Sometimes people would come to speak at school. One time, I remember Natan Sharansky came to speak at school [Lynn's eyes fill with tears]. There's always a *Maccabiyah* (athletic competition) every spring. *(interview, 1994)*

The school seems frozen in time, encased in a glass casket like Sleeping Beauty.

Lynn was looking forward to student teaching the following year, although she was worried about her limitations. She was sure that she would never master enough Talmud to teach Judaic studies in the upper grades and was concerned that her Hebrew wouldn't be good enough, even for upper elementary school. (In fact, Lynn's Hebrew was quite good for an American. She had studied Hebrew all through high school, through four years of college, and would study it an additional two years in graduate school.) What worried her most was classroom management.

> Here's the other piece: I realized a lot of times at camp, it's hard, when you're so close in age to high school kids, to teach them. Sometimes they don't respect you if you're too close to them. Sometimes it works great if you're close to them because you can relate to them. And sometimes you just can't do it because they don't respect you. They say, "Why do I have to listen to you?" I remember when I was in high school and we'd have student teachers from the universities come and teach us. It would be kind of weird having someone three, four years older than us trying to teach us. *(interview, 1994)*

The Struggle of Student Teaching

At the end of her first year, I met with Lynn to set up her student teaching for the spring semester of 1996. Having spent yet another semester learning Jewish texts, Lynn was eager to teach the subjects that she had enjoyed so much to students who would appreciate their subtlety and beauty. She asked to be placed with middle school students. I had my doubts about whether Lynn would project the aura of competence that is so essential to teaching this age group. Yet I also felt that Lynn would be a wonderful role model, especially for the impressionable young women in this age cohort. Lynn was a gifted leader of prayer, someone who appeared, rain or shine, at the Seminary minyan (prayer quorum) wearing her tallit and tefillin. I visited the class of an eighth-grade Bible and Hebrew teacher, a woman highly recommended to me. I thought Lynn's Hebrew skills would be taxed in this class, but I decided, perhaps foolishly (it was early in my career as well as in Lynn's!), to let Lynn decide. True to form, never shrinking from a challenge, she decided to give it her all.

Lynn began her experience, as did all my students, by assessing what she brought to the student teaching experience. She listed her organizational skills, her ability to break down a complex process into a series of smaller skills and steps (something she had encountered while teaching swimming), her ability to relate to her students' lives outside of school, and her creativity (initial self-evaluation, January 12, 1996). In fact, what Lynn had anticipated so eagerly ended up becoming a rather dreadful experience. Lynn never let on in her seminar with me or in her monthly meetings with her supervisor just how bad it was until just before the semester ended.

Lynn's mentor insisted that no English be spoken in her class. "She wouldn't let me explain a word here or there in English because, she said, 'if you do that, the kids will never go back to speaking Hebrew and yadda, yadda, yadda' " *(interview, 1996)*. Poor Lynn had to struggle to make herself understood, trying multiple circumlocutions with a limited Hebrew vocabulary; this process slowed down her lessons and drained from them any vestige of creativity. It was nothing like teaching swimming or teaching Hebrew informally at camp.

> When I was in camp, we'd try to speak Hebrew [in casual conversation], and I'd think that it was great. It's easier to do and less frustrating to do it that way than trying to master the content at the time. Trying to explain what a biblical word means in modern

Hebrew doesn't always come across right. My teacher won't let me say, "This word means this in English" unless I really, really, have to. So one day, I was trying and trying to draw a word out of the kids and kept saying, "Okay, and what else?" and spent maybe two or three minutes trying to get the word out of them. Finally, one girl said in English, "You mean it means this?" And I said [Lynn breathes deeply], "Yes." *(interview, 1996)*

It wasn't like any teaching she had done before, at the Bureau of Jewish Education–sponsored retreats or even at the synagogue school. She was a prisoner of the teacher's intransigent Hebraism, as Suzy had been in her school.

I realized that I didn't teach the same way when I was teaching Hebrew as I did in English because I was too uptight and too tense every time I taught. Sometimes I didn't really think about what I said, so my tenses would be wrong, for example, because I'd be more worried about trying to get the content out in Hebrew and make them understand me. I'd be worried about what I was writing on the board and wondering, "How do I tell this kid to shut up and do everything at once in a language that I can't do everything at once in?" *(interview, 1996)*

Lynn's supervisor never saw the extent of her struggle and tended to dismiss her journal musings as hyperbolic. His reports about her were quite positive. After his initial visit, when he saw her teach a segment of the teacher's prepared lesson, he noted that she did not seem as self-conscious (or self-critical) as she appeared in her journal. "I might also mention that I thought that her Hebrew was quite good" (supervisor's report, February 29, 1996). With each observation, he recorded improvement in her pedagogic technique. But for Lynn, the struggle with Hebrew fluency dominated her teaching. In her final self-evaluation, she delineated Hebrew as her major obstacle and sensed none of the progress that her supervisor or her mentor observed. During her interview, bitterness crept into her voice while discussing the graduate school expectation that she would be able to teach Judaica and Hebraica in Hebrew (*Ivrit b'Ivrit*):

The Seminary expects us to teach *Ivrit b'Ivrit*, but we're not qualified to do it. None of the people I've really talked to feels comfortable doing it. Our mentors aren't always happy with our level of Hebrew, either. Some of us do better than others, but in general there's an overriding feeling that something's not quite right. We're often expected to do something much more than we can handle. *(interview, 1996)*

Lynn's reservations are shared by others in the field. Day school leaders are split between those who demand an all-Hebrew environment as the key to fluency, and those who prefer that students come to grips with the texts in their own language. For the former, the goal is Hebrew literacy; for the latter, the goal is making personal meaning. Lynn's school was staunchly in the *Ivrit b'Ivrit* camp. Her struggle over language eclipsed many of her good intentions and talents. She had to scrap creativity for lack of vocabulary; she couldn't relate to students as she had hoped because it required the ability to schmooze in Hebrew.

The clash between the school's goals and her own compounded Lynn's insecurities. What her school valued was teaching *Ivrit b'Ivrit* and having well-behaved students. Whereas her mentor relied on passive seat-work and whole-group instruction, Lynn had come to student teaching committed to interactive activities and personal meaning-making. In addition to her reservations about the kind of instruction in her mentor's classroom, Lynn was horrified by the way that prayer services were conducted at her school. She was itching to lead them, camp-style, with rousing melodies and more group participation, but had to take a backseat to an Israeli prayer leader who saw religious services as an adjunct to the Hebrew curriculum. Like the beginner Kelly Klinefelter Lee in *Reflections of First-Year Teachers on School Culture* (Donaldson and Poon, 1999), Lynn's idealism bumped up against a far more conservative school culture. In the wake of this clash, it was her idealism that gave way. The day school was no longer so different from the synagogue school that she had once scorned.

As Lynn struggled with the Hebrew language, classroom discipline became an issue. She noted that her day school experience was not that different from the "bad" synagogue school experience that she had undergone during her senior year in college:

In some ways, the differences between an afternoon school where I taught the seventh grade and the day school where I was teaching eighth grade were really in the background. The kids still goofed off and still didn't want to be there, and they didn't want to be doing x, y, and z, and it didn't matter if it was a day school. It does matter if it's afternoon school because it's not *real* school in some ways, but even to some of the kids in the day school, the Hebrew subjects aren't important in the first place. *(interview, 1996)*

Her fantasy stage was over (Ryan, 1986); she was fighting to survive. As a student in a seminar designed to promote reflective practice on the student teaching experience, Lynn had been assigned the task of preparing a critical incident from the classroom. The incident that she chose is one that depicts the interplay of her concerns for Hebrew accuracy and classroom management. While writing a word on the board, Lynn froze as she pondered its spelling. She mused:

> What was I going to do with all eyes watching me and waiting? I made my decision in a split second and continued writing. I had to keep writing, I told myself. I was the teacher, and this student was expecting me to write her suggestion on the board along with everyone else's. I felt compelled to keep writing and pretend I knew what I was doing. How could I stop writing mid-sentence? What would it look like to the students? If I made a major mistake or if it looked like I was not confident, then in their eyes I would be finished as a teacher and role model for them. If I stopped and faced them suddenly and decided not to finish the list on the board, they would have known that I couldn't finish the list, and their behavior toward me would have changed. I did not want that to happen. I did not want to be seen as an "easy" teacher, as someone who they could "goof off" in front of and get away with it. In addition, had I hesitated too long on the board, not only would there have been a dangerous silence for chaos to start in the class while my back was turned, but I, too, would have lost confidence in my ability to teach at this level. (Lynn's case study, 1996)

These are the classic concerns of a novice teacher as described by Britzman (1986). Lynn was convinced that everything depends on the teacher, that all hell would break loose if she was not in control ("a dangerous silence for chaos to start . . . while my back was turned"). She expected that polished teachers could never have gaps in their knowledge. She felt that she was a fraud because she didn't know which of the three Hebrew silent consonants to use in spelling her word. Last, she was convinced that teachers are self-made: she just doesn't have what she would later refer to as "stage presence" and never would. She couldn't imagine that a teacher persona might be crafted over time.

It is important to note that Lynn taught formally only one year, the dreadful experience of teaching during her senior year in college. Unlike Suzy and Nehama, she never had a backlog of experience built up in college and graduate school. Lynn suggested that she probably had made a mistake not taking a part-time job teaching in a synagogue school while in graduate school, as nearly all her fellow students had. She was also hampered by another cultural myth: that day school students would be serious about their Jewish studies—that they would, in fact, be like Lynn. Buchmann (1987) describes this myth, which is common to novice teachers: "Being drawn to schools themselves, intending [sic] teachers may assume that schooling fits naturally into the lives of students who have an aptitude for learning" (p. 160).

Lynn's frustrations came to a head as the semester was coming to a close. She had left the week before Passover to celebrate the holiday with her family in Israel. She came back to a master's thesis that had to be completed, an exam in Talmud, and a lesson to prepare for her final observation by her supervisor. Describing the events that ensued, Lynn reported, "I was under so much stress that Wednesday night and Thursday morning. . . . I basically snapped." During our interview, she used the word "snapped" three times in two minutes.

Lynn stayed up planning a lesson until 2 a.m. Thursday; she then discussed the lesson with her mentor, who asked her to pare it down.

> I was so frustrated because this was another example of my having a great idea, and [my mentor] tried to take it and make it simpler. . . . She said that if you did your own lesson plan it would be okay, but I didn't get the feeling that she really wanted me to do the lesson plan even though she would have let me. She didn't really want me to do it partly because she didn't want me to fail. (interview, 1996)

Lynn's comment was revealing. She understood that her mentor was trying to protect her from failure, yet she was convinced that she would fail, anyway, because of the language problem and, worse still, fail in a lesson that she didn't own. All her options led to one path: failure. (She had explained that her mentor was teaching the eighth grade for the first time, without a curriculum or a cache of lesson plans. Planning with Lynn was mostly dividing up biblical verses between them. The goal was translation of biblical Hebrew into modern Hebrew.)

On Wednesday night, racing against the clock to prepare the lesson, Lynn blew up at her roommates. "I was miserable," she recalls *(interview, 1996)*. On Thursday morning, with only two hours' sleep, she taught the lesson that she originally wanted to teach. "It wasn't any worse than any of my other lessons that failed," she said bitterly *(interview, 1996)*. But what was worse was that in her anger and frustration, Lynn lashed out at her mentor. Lynn recalled the incident with embarrassment:

> I snapped at my teacher. I was so stressed, and it's something I shouldn't have done and something I would normally never have done, even when I disagreed with her. Never, ever. I was *so* rude. She was teaching something that I so disagreed with, and I was still so out of it [from lack of sleep the previous night]. I basically went up to her and said something to the effect that I never would have taught that: "Why did you teach that?" That really was not me. . . . I was so miserable, and she was so taken aback. *(interview, 1996)*

After lunch and a cooling-off period, Lynn apologized, taught her lesson a second time, and came to a new realization: some of her problems with her mentor had to do with the cultural differences that separated them.

More often than not, young American teachers are expected to join a faculty in which large numbers of the faculty are Israeli. Lynn's discomfort at her school's prayer services, led by someone who was unfamiliar with the prayers that her students experienced at their local synagogues or at camp, was a reaction to cultural differences. Her personal discomfort with her mentor was similar.

> *Lynn:* Some of it has to do with her being Israeli and my not being Israeli and picking up on her Israeli idiosyncrasies, which she didn't see and . . .
> *CKI:* Like what? What do you mean by an Israeli idiosyncrasy?
> *Lynn:* Certain mannerisms that she didn't realize she had. [For example,] if I tried to tell her, she'd jump down my throat for saying that she had them.
> *CKI:* Were [the mannerisms] Israeli or were they personal?

Lynn: They could be personal, but it's one that I've noticed in a lot of Israelis. [Lynn backs off a bit, sensing that she's dealing with an ethnic stereotype.] How's that? A couple of my fellow student teachers agreed with me that there were Israeli idiosyncrasies, certain interpersonal kinds of relations, being very abrupt and like, "Do this. Do that." *(interview, 1996)*

Over the course of the year, Lynn also realized that day schools were far more complicated institutions than she had originally envisioned in her first concept map. Her drawing had become much messier, reflecting the fact that teaching can be a messy business.

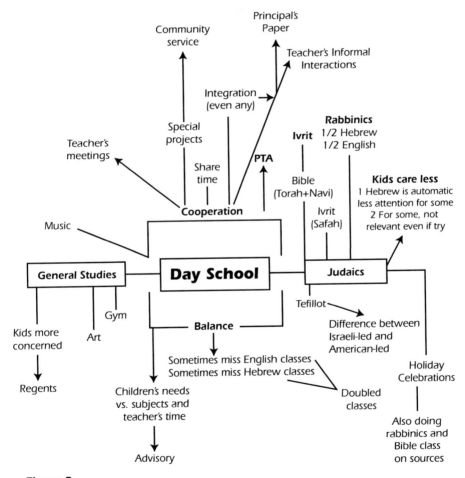

Figure 2

Looking over what she drew and comparing it with her drawing of a year and a half earlier, Lynn observed:

The first thing, looking at my drawing, that comes to mind is that perhaps it's more complex than I had originally imagined or that now I just see more pieces of it, which is probably more realistic. Also, since this was older grades you get to see more of the dynamics than perhaps you would with elementary school, because there's more changing going on in the halls. There's all that dynamic that you would expect in a school with kids running between classes, here and there. I got the feeling that in this school in general, there was a lot of that sort of informal thing—for example, if you had a study hall, someone would ask, "Can I go next door to Mrs. So-and-So's room and grab a dictionary?" or "Can I go to the math room and get this?" "Fine, no problem, go." There were teachers popping in all of a sudden and saying, "Excuse me, can I just make an announcement?"—that happened at least four times a day. "I just need to tell my class—they just left me—that they need to study their math, blah, blah, blah." In some ways, it's nice that the teachers feel comfortable. They can just drop in on each other and do things. Sometimes it's annoying if you're teaching a lesson and people keep popping in and interrupting you, but it also lends something to the atmosphere when teachers feel comfortable doing that. *(interview, 1996)*

Rather than the stark demarcation of general and Jewish studies, a re-creation of a world imagined by a student in and of that world, Lynn's second drawing (Figure 2) introduced new stakeholders, such as parents, PTA, and teachers. She was beginning to think like a professional, showing her understanding of the enterprise as an insider, a member of the faculty. General studies and Judaica were off to the side; the real business of a day school was front and center, what Lynn called "balance." "Balance" meant negotiating who gives way in the face of time pressures: juggling the children's needs versus the needs of the subject or the needs of the teachers. An analogue to "balance" is "cooperation": attempts to integrate subject matter, special projects, such as community service, that extend the curriculum from the school to the wider society, and a synoptic paper written by eighth-graders, called the principal's paper, which was an attempt to span the diverse elements of the curriculum across the Judaic and general studies divide. Lynn's world was a circus, the school as a trapeze, with the teacher/performer desperately trying to keep from falling. Mary Freeman, one of Ryan's (1992) "rookie teachers," describes herself during her first year of teaching as a tightrope walker. Like Lynn's, Freeman's recollections echo her unremitting concentration and sense of immediate danger.

Lynn's concerns over Hebrew language spilled over onto her concept map. Next to her category of Judaics, she added value judgments, instead of the more factual descriptions that characterized the rest of her concept map: "Kids care less." Hebrew is "automatic," demanding less attention for some, and for others, "not relevant, even if [they] try." She does so for *tefillot* as well, another area of her concern. She indicated that there is a "difference between Israeli-led and American-led" prayer. Her bitter disappointment is etched into her drawing.

Lynn's concept map, her interview, and her final self-evaluation all told the same story: that of a dispirited but talented young woman whose student teaching experience left her very wary about the career that she had chosen. When I met with her, she was trying to find a position teaching in a day school in the Midwest, closer to home. In late April, she had no takers and was beginning to consider positions other than in Jewish day schools.

CKI: So, would you be heartbroken if you could not find the right job in a day school at this point?

Lynn: The way things are going now, no. If I could find a good job that I really felt comfortable with, with people I would like working with, in a city [I like], you know. . . . No, I don't think it would [break my heart]. [Finding a teaching position in a day school] would be nice on the one hand, but on the other, if I've found a different job that I really like. . . . If I can't find a day school job, I'm not going to say, "Oh well, I wish I had a day school job" and keep hunting for one.

The First Year of Teaching: Trying to Stay Afloat

By mid-summer 1996, Lynn had found a teaching job in Lakeview, a small city in the Midwest. The day school in Lakeview offered proximity to her family, a less frenetic pace than New York, and an assurance that her spoken Hebrew was adequate for the task. She rejected an offer as an assistant teacher in another school, proposed by the principal as an opportunity for Lynn to improve her Hebrew as she participated in a highly structured internship with a master teacher. Like Nehama, Lynn felt that she deserved a class of her own. Lynn chose Lakeview in order to have that autonomy, even if it meant a pieced-together assignment of teaching two-thirds of the time in a community day school and one-third in the community-sponsored religious school. Another reason for choosing Lakeview was Ben Cohen, the young director of the Bureau of Jewish Education, who was the interviewer who hired her. Lynn felt that they shared a vision of teaching and learning and similar experiences studying under Conservative Jewish auspices and attending Camp Ramah.

The task of supervising the faculty of the day school was divided along the lines of Judaica faculty and general studies faculty. The principal of the day school, Betty Stein, supervised the general studies teachers; Ben Cohen would be Lynn's supervisor, having taken the responsibility of working with the Judaic studies staff because of his familiarity with Hebrew and Jewish texts. Lynn welcomed the opportunity to do both day school and religious school teaching and looked forward to working with Ben.

There were a number of high points during the year. Lynn's students delighted her when they came through—for example, when they finally pulled together an all-Hebrew presentation in a school-wide Hanukkah celebration. Seeing an indifferent or even disruptive student change for the better was a source of great pleasure. Amanda, who was always complaining, "Yuck! Why are we learning Hebrew? This is sooo boring!" asked to take a Haggadah home so that she could lead her family's seder. Danny, who had problems reading in English as well as in Hebrew, began to catch on to Hebrew reading and even asked Lynn for help when his classmates were "goofing off and getting into trouble" (interview, 1997). Marissa, a student in the religious school who in the fall insisted that she didn't want to be there, signed up for another year.

But the low points outnumbered the high. Lynn was "overwhelmed" by the diversity in her classes: native Hebrew speakers whose parents emigrated from Israel, Russian students who had recently arrived in the United States, and the assortment of students with learning disabilities and various forms of attention deficit disorder. Lynn's old bugaboo, classroom management, was once again an issue. The word "challenging" peppered her frustrated and sarcastic 1997 interview:

There are always the lovely class management issues where you start noticing kids throwing pencils at each other for no particular reason. What can you do that will mean something to them to get them to stop? There have been a lot of those sorts of challenges. My third grade—I only have five children—has three boys and two girls, so there is usually one boy who's almost always feeling left out. So that became a creative problem-solving issue. How do we do group things where they can all get along, where we're not going to come in off recess every day with them fighting or complaining about who didn't play with whom? So it's been a very interesting year. Five kids, and it's a lot of work. (*interview, 1997*)

Lynn sent unruly children to the principal's office; according to her, the principal never asked what was going on in her class. When Lynn asked directly for advice, the principal would recommend a parent conference that brought about limited changes in the student's behavior. In place of the absentee supervisor, Lynn's mother and her coterie of teacher friends became Lynn's unofficial mentors, offering suggestions for controlling students' inappropriate behavior. Lynn tried writing misbehaving students' names on the blackboard, or writing class rules on multicolored index cards that she would distribute to rule breakers. The students soon turned collecting cards into a game. She tried rewarding positive behavior through stars and prizes. She offered time in a comfy beanbag chair for students who behaved appropriately.

The literature about novice teachers is studded with similar stories. Control looms large as a central issue. Somewhere there is an answer, the holy grail of classroom management. The novice hunts for recipes, for what works (Britzman, 1986; Kagan, 1992). In their absence, the novice is stuck in what Ryan (1986) calls the survival stage, just hanging on day after day.

Another theme in the literature of novices is that the teacher feels let down and blames others. In Stark's (1991) account of a beginning teacher, Kim becomes anxious about her ability to teach a particularly difficult group of youngsters. "No one sat down with me and told me exactly what was expected. . . . It is the department; they are not social with anyone. . . . Someone should have said, 'Can you come so I can explain everything?' " (pp. 303–4). Lynn's colleagues were not very helpful in offering her advice about teaching. They taught part-time and dashed off after class to other engagements. There were few staff meetings.

When Lynn was told what was expected, it presumed a mastery by students that didn't square with Lynn's assessment of what the students knew. She was wary about getting off on the wrong foot with the woman who had taught her class the previous year. The wife of a local Orthodox rabbi who knew the students from the community, this teacher prided herself on, according to Lynn, "racing through the *Tal Sela* curriculum [a Hebrew language program for the elementary grades in a day school] just to get done with it." Lynn was astounded at how poor her students' Hebrew skills were. "I wanted to slow down and make sure that they studied fewer words, so they could actually know them" *(interview, 1997).*

I got my curriculum over the summer, so I spent a lot of time looking through the first book and I planned out all the stuff. After the first week, when I had done a little bit of review, thinking that this is where they finished last year, I realized that I couldn't do this because not only was it after the summer and they had forgotten the material, but they'd been taught past tense and present tense and whatever before, but none of it stuck in their brains. It was sort of like we had to go back and start over again. In the beginning of the year, I was so befuddled, and I didn't want to share that with other people. *(interview, 1997)*

While student teaching, Lynn bought into her mentor's vision of teaching Hebrew and Bible without voicing her disagreement, except for that one moment when she "snapped." During her first year of teaching, she learned to tinker with the curriculum based on what her students seemed to need. She adapted it, borrowing other resources from Ben Cohen's bookshelves. Zeichner and Tabachnick (1985) note these patterns in their studies of student teachers who become first-year teachers. Lynn moved from what they call "strategic compliance," harboring private reservations about the efficacy of certain practices but outwardly buying in to the curricular goals, to "strategic redefinition," attempts to widen the instructional parameters through negotiation (pp. 9–10). Lynn told Ben, but no one else, that she couldn't teach *Tal Sela* without making changes to suit her students' real level of mastery. Having a class of her own freed Lynn from being bound to curricular expectations with which she neither agreed nor was a party to creating.

Lynn wanted supervision, but it appears that she fell between the institutional cracks. The principal of the day school, as in many small day schools, was from the world of general education. Betty was not assigned to supervise Lynn because she knew no Hebrew. Ben, the director of the Bureau of Jewish Education, who did know Hebrew, became too busy with his bureau responsibilities to help Lynn, whom he had hired for her youth, her commitment to constructivist pedagogy, and her zeal. Apparently, there were complaints about Lynn being "mean" from a parent who was president of the board. Although Lynn saw Ben as her protector, she was aware on some level of her precarious position.

> I had both of [the board president's] children—one in each of
> my classes—and she would say things periodically to the direc-
> tor of the bureau. He would listen, but it had obviously been his
> decision—not hers—to hire me, and how he thought I was
> doing was important. But it was very hard because it's a small
> community. I had trouble and was afraid to do anything. *(inter-
> view, 1997)*

Stone (1987) comments on the isolation of new teachers. They often don't have mentors or helpful colleagues, and even if there is a supervisor, novices are afraid to reveal how difficult their lives are.

In April, Betty asked Lynn to take over a second and fourth grade so that she could observe her teaching. (This was the first time that Betty had observed her.) These were the grades that Betty was considering assigning to Lynn in the coming year. Lynn felt that the teaching went well. The fourth-graders loved the song that she taught them and listened patiently to the story that she told them. "Even if they weren't motivated, the kids who didn't want to pay attention were quiet about it" *(interview, 1997)*. She really enjoyed teaching that class. "I was having a wonderful time and came out thinking, 'Wow! I'll teach this class next year' " *(interview, 1997)*.

At the post-observation meeting, Lynn had the rug pulled out from underneath her. Betty and Ben were both there. Betty began with her concerns about Lynn's classroom management. Lynn recalls her vote of no confidence:

She said to me, "You know, I can see that there will still be some students who will give you trouble," and then proceeded to tell me that she still thought I'd potentially have class management problems with this class next year. *(interview, 1997)*

Betty's words stung, even though Ben seemed more confident about Lynn's ability to make it. He knew that she had been having trouble all along and was willing to help her as much as he could, given his multiple commitments. Lynn felt that if she decided to stay for another year, Ben would find money to send her to Israel and to take educational classes at the university. He offered her a limited schedule for the coming academic year, maybe one class in the preschool or kindergarten, where there would be less pressure. But in Lynn's mind, Betty's negativity outweighed Ben's support.

I suspect that it was Betty, not Ben, who had to deal with parents, especially the angry president of the board. She had to listen to complaints that Lynn was "mean"; she saw the exiles from Lynn's classroom sitting in her office. Weinstein (1989) notes that preservice teachers are much more likely to be interested in the affective domain of teaching, in enhancing their students' self-esteem and having their students like them. Their descriptions of what makes for good teaching omit domains such as having learners "acquire subject matter understanding, strategies for learning, or some other form of content" (p. 58). Lynn's aims in teaching were not like those of Weinstein's novices: her first priority was teaching Torah, which may not have been the first priority of the parents of the school. Lynn probably spent too little time on the affective domain—making allies of her students. This is no real surprise; Lynn's first priority, as we have seen in examining her implicit theories, was always teaching Torah. She was impatient with those who didn't share her love of learning. Lynn's situation was complicated by the division of labor that Betty and Ben had created. Last, since it hadn't been Betty who had made the decision to hire Lynn, Betty felt less loyalty toward her than Ben did.

The frustrations of the year were manifest in Lynn's concept map (Figure 3) drawn in 1997. In her struggle (a word she incorporates into her concept map to establish authority), she reverted to an old-fashioned notion of teacher as disseminator of information and policeman, alongside her more progressive notions of teaching (teacher as guide and as role model). She had become jaded by the students' lack of interest in what interested her ("Do well only when interested in activity") and by the parents' lack of commitment ("Place to drop kids daily").

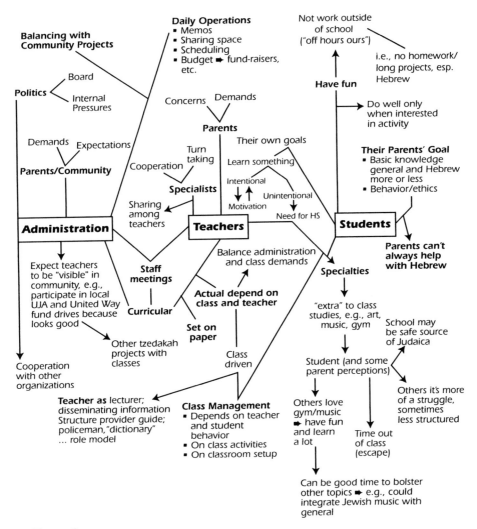

Figure 3

While her enthusiasm was eroding, the school administration demanded more than teaching: participation in UJA and United Way fund drives.

The meeting with Betty and Ben convinced Lynn to leave the community and look for another teaching position in a day school. "Her comments so got to me, on top of not being happy in the community, anyway. I'm just going to bail and find myself a more comfortable atmosphere" *(interview, 1997).* A more comfortable atmosphere meant a larger commu-

nity with more social opportunities for young singles as well more professional resources: a school that offered more supervision and tutoring.

> I'll try day school again at least for another year, hopefully for
> two or three. Then if I'm still really struggling and as miserable
> as I was this year despite my best efforts to change, I'll stop and
> look back and say, "Well, maybe I don't want to do this."
> Maybe I should go back and look for the things I liked, such as
> camp, and go back and start over that way. *(interview, 1997)*

What was significant about Lynn's remarks at the close of a difficult
year was not her determination to make it in this career. As Lynn's portraitist, I have had more than ample evidence of this determination: the
young girl who wanted a meaningful bat mitzvah, the student who was
determined to teach *Ivrit b'Ivrit*. What was striking was a recognition
that her problems might not be completely attributable to the failure of
her graduate program to prepare her properly, or a rigid mentor, or an
administrator who assigned her to a difficult class, or the diversity of
the students, or the lack of professional resources such as personnel to
supervise her or aides to teach students with special needs. Lynn was
thinking about her own need to change.

Subsequent Teaching Experiences

Stung by her experience in Lakeview, Lynn readily accepted the offer
that she received late in June: to teach third grade in a suburban area
outside of New York, in the town of Bondville. What was appealing
was the promise of a larger school with a collegial faculty, access to a
bigger Jewish community, and an assignment that might help her
change: teaching half the day in her own third-grade Hebrew class and
being an aide for the rest of the day in a first-grade Hebrew class with a
seasoned teacher. An additional incentive was the promise of support
from a caring principal. The principal, Rachel Cooper, allowed Lynn to
stay with her until she found her own apartment in a nearby community. Remembering her, Lynn was profoundly grateful:

> She gave me such wonderful help and guidance. When she came
> to observe me in the classroom—granted, she did have plenty of

criticisms—her report was broken down: "These are the things that you do well. These are the things that could be worked on. These are the things that you really need to change now." But it was always tempered by something like, "Okay, you're doing this. You could do it better this way." It was a very fair critique, and it was always attached with several suggestions about how to improve. The tone was very positive. *(interview, 1999)*

As she was being rehired for a second year to teach one section of the third-grade Judaica curriculum and to be an aide in a third-grade general studies class, Lynn found out that Rachel would be leaving. The new principal was beset with personal problems—an ailing father and a bout with her own serious illness. Supervision evaporated to one formal observation. Lynn described feeling "very negative" after her post-observation conference with the principal:

I walked in and said, "Okay, I know that this and this went wrong in that lesson because I didn't have enough *Haggadot*, and my kids didn't want to share, and that created a mess." The critique that I got was much more critical, much more harsh. It was sort of like, "You have a lot of potential, you're young, you'll learn a lot, and you're going to be a great teacher, but you're not doing anything right now." This is how I felt.

She didn't give me specific suggestions, such as "Go watch so-and-so," whereas my previous principal had suggested, "Try this, try that, and if you want, watch so-and-so." I didn't get that feeling and that support from the principal who observed me this year. *(interview, 1999)*

Lynn was troubled by the dissonance in the messages that the principal gave her. Although her words conveyed a sense of Lynn's potential, the music behind them was not upbeat. In his article "The Good Mentor," Rowley (1999) describes the quality that Lynn missed in the principal's message: good mentor teachers capitalize on opportunities to affirm the human potential of their mentees. They do so in private conversations and in public settings. Good mentors share their own struggles and frustrations and how they overcame them. And always, they do so in a genuine and caring way that engenders trust (p. 22).

Lynn was still haunted by the elusiveness of the "teacher persona," the ability to command the attention of a class. In the final self-evaluation that she completed after student teaching, she commented on her need to work on "stage presence." Three years later, she was still aware of its absence and still feeling like a novice.

> You know, there are times when I walk in and if another teacher is a guest in my classroom—maybe just because it's a different person and it's not me—all of a sudden I notice that the kids are quiet. I'm like, "Why? Why don't they do this for me?" *(interview, 1999)*

Lynn had yet to acquire the "practical knowledge" that seasoned teachers have. Evoking Elbaz (1983), Fenstermacher (1994) re-creates the contours of that knowledge: the rules of practice (what to do in certain situations); practical principles such as how to organize one's knowledge for learners; and images—metaphors, vignettes, jokes, and other ways to build verbal bridges to one's students. Reviewing the ways that experts perceive classroom situations, decode signs, and re-configure their teaching as a result (Bransford et al., 2000), one is struck by what Lynn was missing.

Although the second year in the Bondville Day School was easier because Lynn knew the subject matter, she was troubled by her students' rowdiness, their poor social skills, and the diversity of their needs. Her concept map (Figure 4) drawn in 1999 indicated their insatiability: she was forced to play the roles of "Mommy," "Police," "Nurse," and "Tutor." The children's moods seemed inexplicable, and this capriciousness dominated her thoughts about them. She listed "depends on moods" twice. "Behavior," both inside and outside the classroom, was the only attribute that Lynn included under the category of students. She was unable to establish a connection to them and to parlay that connection to an attachment to Jewish learning. Like most novice teachers, Lynn had many clerical duties, something she listed in her relationships with the "Office." Her relationships with parents were ambivalent. By adding the question mark in "Compliments?" Lynn has added a note of irony as well. Far more frequent are "Complaints" and "Demands," although Lynn respected the fact that she got "Ideas" as well.

What made the years in Bondville easier to bear was something that was lacking in the school in Lakeview: warm colleagues in whom she could confide.

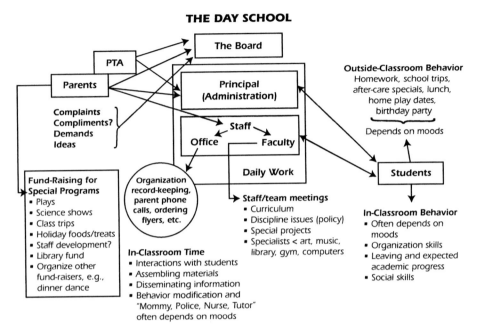

Figure 4

Yesterday I had a horrible day. Then one of my co-teachers from the English class and I went out Rollerblading for an hour and a half and gabbed and let go. It was such a wonderful feeling because I didn't have that where I was [in Lakeview], and I didn't have it even when I did my student teaching. It makes a difference. *(interview, 1999)*

A new theme emerged in this 1999 interview with Lynn: her concern for moral education as well cultural literacy and mastery of content matter. One of the few successes that Lynn recalled (she is far more ready to discuss her failures) was when a child who could barely read served as prayer leader. Her students, always ready to pick on one another, behaved beautifully: "Nobody criticized him for reading slowly and stumbling through the words. Nobody laughed. They all told him he did a nice job." Building a moral community in which each member was respected was a priority. The lack of that community was painful to Lynn. It was what she had hoped to find in a Jewish day school. The lack of parental role models was another source of pain. Lynn described parents who were involved in their respective careers, "parents who don't come home until 8 or 9 at night" *(interview, 1999)*:

> As soon as you meet the parents, you're like, now I know why the kid is so rude. Because the parent is being rude at conferences, and you can see it. You feel like you're talking to a brick wall. You're trying to teach [the children] values, and you're trying to show them that you know all the things we keep quoting from *Pirke Avot* [*Ethics of the Fathers*] or about *V'ahavta l're'akha kamokha* [You should love your neighbor as yourself]—those sorts of things. They don't get it at home, so why should they listen to me tell them that that is how to behave? It's very frustrating from that standpoint. I didn't expect to have that [disconnect between home and school]. I really thought, oh, it's a day school. It should be better. *(interview, 1999)*

Once again, Lynn, like Kim in Stark's (1991) account and so many other teachers, both novices and veterans, dealt with her professional disappointment by blaming the parents.

What Lynn meant by moral education can be found in the word "restraint." She was hoping that her students could conform their behavior to the vision of morality communicated in biblical and rabbinic literature, or the one promulgated by the nineteenth-century founders of the American "common" school. Her views, as pointed out by James Davison Hunter in *The Death of Character* (2001), were not really about children but an idealized view of what she expected of adults. If the parents' behavior was narcissistic and indulgent, no wonder the children reflected such rudeness and "willfulness," the favorite word of early-nineteenth-century moral education. It was no surprise that in her 1999 concept map, Lynn referred to one of the teacher's functions as "Police." Her view of moral education was that of Durkheim (1973): moral education begins with the internalization of society's norms and obedience to them. Moral education was about heteronomy, not autonomy. Lynn's concept map refers to class time as the locus of "disseminating information" and "behavior modification," another retreat from the language of progressive education that she had learned as a graduate student.

Another change in Lynn's thinking about day school education was her growing appreciation for integration across subject-matter lines.

Teaching both Judaic studies and general studies during her second year in Bondville made Lynn relish the opportunities for collaboration within the faculty. She was pleased to participate in a field trip to see a play about Helen Keller, which was the culmination of a unit on disabilities in general studies and her teaching in *Humash* about the nearly blind Isaac, exploited by Jacob at his mother's urging. Although she made passing references to the subject in her earlier interviews, it loomed large in her 1999 interview. Like Nehama, whose views about curriculum changed while working with the teacher who was in charge of cocurricular education, Lynn formed her newer views of integration because of a new context for her teaching. She thought about team teaching with a friend, a general studies teacher:

> We had proposed, had I stayed here, that the two of us would take one class and stay all day together. She'd take the lead for English and write the lesson plans, and I would take the lead in Hebrew and she could help me. I was thinking, "Wow, that would be fabulous!" *(interview, 1999)*

But that was not to be. Lynn moved on once again, looking for a community that was less suburban, with more people her own age. She looked southward, to a bustling city in which her sister lived, and found a position teaching second grade in the Merryvale Schechter Day School. A novice can handle professional disappointment if she is personally satisfied. Lynn was not.

Although I didn't formally interview Lynn that year, we stayed in touch by telephone. During the year, I spoke to her principal and asked how Lynn was doing. She told me that Lynn was having difficulty. The Judaic studies coordinator was working with her and had paired Lynn with another second-grade teacher. The principal mentioned that Lynn's subject-matter expertise, her Hebrew, and her commitment to Jewish practice were great strengths. She said, "If only she would smile." This was a comment that Rachel Cooper, Lynn's principal in Bondville, had made to me; it was something I had said to Lynn when I visited her class in Bondville. Lynn acknowledged this problem in her e-mails to me:

> I think part of my problem also is that I'm not a good actor. After twenty minutes of their nonsense, it's hard for me to still be smiling and not take it personally. . . . I try to be cheerful and

enthusiastic, but rarely can I keep it up for the whole two hours. (personal communication, February 12, 1997)

In the spring of 2000, the Judaic studies coordinator in Merryvale counseled Lynn to leave day school education. She felt that Lynn just wasn't connecting to her students. Lynn did so, and after a short stint at a national Jewish women's organization, she found a position working for a national youth group. In April 2001, she wrote me:

I'm really enjoying my work. I can write creative programs and help my high schoolers write educational activities. It's more relaxing than teaching—even when we have a string of conventions in a row. I also feel more freedom to express thoughts and "teach" the way I think is best, as opposed to last year. And I feel appreciated. Often last year, I felt only the criticism. ("Why don't you teach this instead? Look at how X does it.") This year, there is more of the positive. Maybe someday I'll return to teaching (perhaps not until I marry and have kids), but for now I'm happy doing informal education. (personal communication)

Epilogue

Lynn was still in Merryvale and had worked with the youth movement for two years, when she was let go because of budget cuts. The Al Aqsa intifada had destroyed a good deal of what she was hired to do: arrange trips to Israel for teenagers. She really loved the work and was sad to leave. She then worked for a JCC teaching Hebrew and adult education. Once again, she locked horns with a supervisor. As Lynn put it, "My boss and I didn't see eye to eye" (telephone interview, June 16, 2004). There were productivity issues; the supervisor expected more and more, even as Lynn succeeded in achieving the goals she had been set. Lynn commented on the differences between teaching in a day school and doing this kind of work. Discipline still figures largely in her discussion.

I always enjoyed informal education. I'm better suited for it. I can control two hundred people at a convention, but I couldn't seem to control twenty [in my own class]. I could be more relaxed; I was perceived in a different light. I had no need to be an authority figure. There was no principal above me, forcing me to do things I didn't like. It's a few days, that's all. The same with adult education: it's somewhat more relaxed, so I did better. In my day school teaching, expectations were always higher and unreasonable. I literally made myself sick from stress. I just couldn't please my supervisor. Parents wouldn't get their kids tested, or they just didn't care. In a class of four students, all of them had big problems. I had a kid who simply couldn't spell, but the supervisor wouldn't make any modifications in the class expectations. (telephone interview, June 16, 2004)

This was the first time I recalled that Lynn, like Suzy and Nehama, had gotten sick "from" teaching as well as sick "of" teaching.

During the year that she taught at the JCC, a friend approached Lynn about teaching in a Jewish day high school. She considered it. It would be a very different context, a more limited subject matter—"only Bible, only Hebrew, or courses that would be taught in English. But I didn't want to go there. I have too much respect for the people who are doing the work there." Lynn's anxiety about day school teaching had not abated over time.

Now she was considering a very different career. She was returning to her hometown to begin a program leading to a master's degree in nursing, another caring career. She thought that she might teach in a synagogue school while doing her course work. As Biklen (1986) observed, once a teacher, always a teacher. After the rigidity of day school life, synagogue school actually looked good to Lynn. "In Hebrew school, I'm a solo practitioner—I can make the modifications. I wish I had discovered this earlier" (telephone conversation, June 16, 2004). She had completely reversed her views on the superiority of a day school education over that of the synagogue school.

Weinstein's observations about novice teachers' preconceptions apply to Lynn. She entered the field with a sense of herself as a teacher that convinced her that she would have no difficulty. (Lynn pointed to her success as a swimming teacher.) She also assumed that she understood day schools because she had attended one. The students would be eager learners, and since she had studied both Jewish education and Bible, among other disciplines, she was equipped to teach. Weinstein refers to the "unrealistic optimism" of new teachers (1989,

p. 54). Novices leave when their expectations do not match up to reality.

Lynn held three jobs in three years, after leaving day school teaching. I found myself wondering how much of this was about the precarious life of Jewish communal professionals in hard economic times, and how much of this was Lynn. Meanwhile, like Elvis, Lynn had left the building.

CHAPTER FIVE
Conclusions

I began my study ten years ago by enlisting the support of three prospective day school teachers in helping me to answer the following research questions:

- What are the professional journeys of novice day school teachers?
- How do these novice teachers understand the function and functioning of Jewish day schools?
- How do they understand their role within this culture?
- How, if at all, do their perceptions change over time?

My plan was to interview Suzy, Nehama, and Lynn from their entry into a graduate program of Jewish education, through student teaching, their first year in a full-time teaching position, and over their first three years in the field. As Nehama wryly noted, "Man plans, and God laughs." My plan changed because my collaborators changed their plans. Within three years of their entry into the field of day school teaching, each of the three had decided to leave day school education. My portraits had to adapt; in addition to being a study of the perceptions of young teachers, my book became an analysis of teacher attrition.

The Journeys

In the obituary he wrote about Eudora Welty, *New York Times* reporter Albin Krebs shared with his readers Welty's interest in stories. "Long before I wrote stories, I listened for stories. . . . Listening *for* them is something more acute than listening *to* them. I suppose it's an early form of participation in what goes on" (2001, C22). Listening for the stories in their teacher talk made me an active partner in the experiences of Suzy, Nehama, and Lynn. What I learned about them from this participation makes up the content of this chapter. Suzy, Nehama, and Lynn seemed to have many of the qualities that Campbell (1990–91) identifies as characteristics of the expert teacher. These are qualities that would predict a long and successful career in Jewish day school education. All three brought remarkably similar "private views" (Buchmann, 1987) and crucial early experiences to their work as day school teachers. The products of day schools themselves, they were raised in homes where their parents, all professionals, were actively involved in the world of education. For Suzy and Lynn, watching their parents toil in the Jewish community as lay leaders was a constant in their childhood. Lynn and Nehama each had one parent who worked in schools. Nehama's stepfather was a paraprofessional in the public school system; and Lynn's mother taught general studies in a community day school.

All three participated in Jewish youth movements as teenagers, went to Jewish camps, and visited Israel. They made up their minds to enter Jewish education while they were in college (although Lynn found a memento from a middle school party in which her friends had predicted that she would become a teacher). Campbell (1990–91) reports that another factor in the personal histories of expert teachers is that they were supported in their career choices by significant others in their lives. My three respondents were all encouraged by their parents in their choice of professions. When I asked each of the three if their parents would have been equally supportive of their career choice had they been male, each of the three immediately responded in the affirmative. Nehama, who became engaged and married during the early years of the study, chose as her spouse a man who made his career in day school teaching.

Each took courses in Jewish studies during her college experience: Nehama majored in Jewish studies, while Suzy and Lynn did considerable course work in the field, just shy of majoring in it. For all three, a positive experience in a Lainer internship sponsored by JESNA (Jewish Educational Services of North America) during their junior year in Israel helped to clarify their career goals. While in Israel, they participated in a course entitled "Issues in American Jewish Education," met Jewish educators, and visited Jewish educational settings. As Lainer interns, they then undertook a year of supervised employment in an educational setting arranged by JESNA. All three taught in religious schools for varying amounts of time, from one year in college to four years of college and graduate school.

Campbell (1990–91) also learned that expert teachers demonstrate early in their preservice teaching the desire to improve their teaching. Suzy and Lynn chose to spend time (and their own resources) on improving their Hebrew fluency by studying in Israel in *ulpanim* (language immersion programs). Nehama paid to take a course in the teaching of reading to help her do a better job in an arena for which she was not prepared. Another factor that Campbell cites is the commitment to improve one's teaching. Suzy, Nehama, and Lynn all demonstrated this commitment to the craft of teaching: in a search for better materials (Suzy), more child-centered teaching (Nehama), and more effective techniques for classroom management (Lynn).

A final factor that Campbell (1990–91) notes is the sense of mission. For each of the three women with whom I collaborated, teaching in a Jewish day school was an opportunity to connect with the Jewish community. Although each considered other arenas of Jewish education at some point in her college and graduate school years, the three decided that Jewish day schools were the most powerful vehicle for realizing this connectedness. For Nehama, teaching in a Jewish day school was a way of acknowledging that the education that she received as a youngster—and didn't fully appreciate at that time—was valuable. In addition, it was a means of ensuring that young people would receive the education that her siblings did not receive. For Suzy, it was being part of a world in which she felt at home as a member of a majority, instead of a minority, culture. For Lynn, it was the appeal of introducing students to the texts she loved, to prayer, and to observance. Although none of them uses the word "vocation" in her interviews, each describes her professional choice as if teaching in a day school were an obligation, a form of compensation or contribution to the community, as well as an avenue of self-actualization. To summarize, each had what Campbell (1990–91) describes as that special relationship between her teaching and her personal value system, "including religious or spiritual belief" (p. 36). Each also ascribed to Campbell's "holistic view of teaching" (p. 37). It was not enough to find Jewish education personally meaningful; part of their mission was to make it meaningful to the students they taught. To paraphrase the title of a sadly out-of-print volume edited by my colleagues Michael Zeldin and Sara Lee (1995), each wanted to touch the future.

In her study of why new teachers go into the profession, Wadsworth (2001) analyzes the responses of 664 public school teachers and 250 private school teachers who had been in the classroom for five years or less. Despite the long hours and low pay, her respondents saw teaching as an opportunity to engage in an enterprise with a transcendent nature. They were called, as were Suzy, Nehama, and Lynn, to do big, important, life-affirming work. Their ideas of what this work entails differ: to nurture (Suzy), to pay back the Jewish community in a meaningful way (Nehama), or to transmit cultural norms (Lynn). The teachers in Wadsworth's study stayed in teaching because they enjoyed it. As one of her respondents reported, "I don't want to do a job that I don't like and don't have fun with" (p. 25). Williams (2003), studying twelve stellar teachers who had remained in teaching for at least fifteen years, came to a similar set of conclusions. Personal fulfillment was inseparable from professional fulfillment. "For these teachers, doing work that feels good goes hand in hand with doing good work" (p. 74).

For Suzy, Nehama, and Lynn, the fun seeped out of their work as their morale was sapped. Despite the personal and experiential factors that would have predicted longevity in the field, all three of my respondents left it. Nehama left day school teaching in the middle of her second year as an assistant teacher, never having received a class of her own. (She continued teaching in religious school for two more years.) In June 2001, she left Jewish education to become a full-time mother. After a brief hiatus, she began to tiptoe back in, leading children's services and working in a Jewish day camp. Suzy left after her third year of full-time teaching, having first worked as a substitute in another day school for an additional semester. She is now working in a large communal agency, noting that she's doing Jewish education "through the back door." Lynn left after four years, spent in three different day schools. After designing curriculum and educational programs for a national Jewish youth organization and teaching adult education in a JCC, she has applied and been accepted to nursing school. She thinks that she will probably teach in a synagogue school on a very part-time basis during the course of her nursing studies.

In her interview with David Berliner, a leading researcher of expertise in teaching, Scherer (2001) reminds her readers that it takes five to eight years to master the craft. Using Scherer and Berliner's figure, all three of my collaborators left before this point in their careers, or in what Sharon Feiman-Nemser (1983) refers to as the "survival stage." Like 39% of new teachers, Lynn, Suzy, and Nehama left within five years (Heller, 2004, p. 5).

All three had a difficult first year. Citing a request for proposals of the National Institute of Education in 1978, Feiman-Nemser (1983) repeats the assumption of the research grant: "The first year of teaching [has] a strong influence on the level of effectiveness which that teacher is able to achieve and sustain over the years" (p. 158). Whether it had bearing on their effectiveness is difficult to assess. But that first year surely had an impact on how my collaborators thought about teaching. Their sense of personal efficacy was jolted, and since being a teacher was at the very center of who they were, each felt frustration and unease. Suzy confided that only because I had advised her and her classmates to think of their entry into day school teaching as a two-year induction did she come back for a second year.

None of the three experienced the "fantasy" stage of Ryan's (1986) first-year teachers; there was no honeymoon period after student teaching. Knowing that they would have to teach in Hebrew served as a brake on overweening self-confidence. In addition, Lynn most assuredly—and Suzy, somewhat less so—felt let down by her student teaching experience. Because of these factors, all three skipped over the "fantasy" stage in Ryan's paradigm, landing squarely in the "survival" stage. During that first year, all three missed a key element in the professional career of successful teachers: working with colleagues who supported them, listened to them, and solved problems with them. Campbell (1990–91) describes this essential element as the peer support system (p. 37). Although Suzy had friends among members of the faculty, she didn't click with the teacher with whom she was paired. Nehama, too, was caught up in the skirmishes of a mismatched team. Lynn had to turn to her day school teacher mother, and her mother's colleagues, to find the collegiality she sought among the busy, part-time faculty of Lakeview. Although Grossman and Richert (1996) refer to preservice teachers, their comments on the need for community and collegiality seem equally true of my three respondents. "Schools as they currently exist reinforce the practice of teaching as a soloist, rather than as a member of an ensemble" (p. 203). Lynn was surely hungry for supportive colleagues and left to flounder. Even in the schools with team teaching, the "ensembles" existed in name only. Pollak and Mills (1997) remind us that successful team teaching doesn't happen on its own. Both Suzy and Nehama suffered, as members of ill-functioning teams, the isolation that Lynn felt as a solo teacher. This isolation is one reason that beginning teachers leave the profession (Stone, 1987; Perez, Swain & Hartsough, 1997).

A concomitant theme in the "teacher talk" I heard was how all three teachers felt let down by their administrators during that crucial first year. Suzy, who was teaching in a new school, understood that her supervisors were overwhelmed with keeping parents happy, building a board, recruiting new students, and trying to find a new building. But she still needed their help. Nehama kept expecting the administration to sit down with her sparring co-teachers and help them straighten out their issues. That help never arrived. For Lynn, there was only a modicum of supervision, and when it was finally offered, late in the year by Betty Stein, it was delivered without that message of hope and optimism that Rowley (1999) notes as essential to good mentoring. All three suffered, in varying degrees, crises in their self-confidence that affected their sense of self. Campbell (1990–91) reminds us that experts are able to function in difficult situations knowing that they are respected; their strong sense of professional autonomy allows them to fulfill their mission despite a difficult work environment. Novices need hand-holding from a caring administration. In discussing the nexus of the personal and professional, Zimmerman (2003) cautions her readers:

> New teachers need mentors and opportunities for professional development, yes, but more important, they need an ongoing celebration of their willingness to struggle and survive through the frustrations and disappointments of first-year [and, I would add, subsequent years—CKI] teaching. And they need to know that just by surviving, they have made a difference. (p. 77)

In an important study conducted by the Public Education Network (PEN; 2003), researchers asked new teachers what their most pressing workplace issues were. I have noted where these themes appear in the narratives of my collaborators as well.

- Large classes
- Insufficient classroom space or no assigned classroom
- Lack of basic resources or materials such as books, textbooks, or supplies, or not knowing what resources were available (Suzy, Lynn)
- Lack of a strong professional community or culture (Suzy, Nehama, Lynn)
- Weak or preoccupied leadership (Suzy, Nehama, Lynn)
- Discipline issues (Lynn)

- Not knowing what to expect; having to learn things the hard way (Suzy, Lynn) (p. 22)

There are no similar large-scale studies of Jewish day school teachers. Kelner, Rabkin, Saxe, and Sheingold (2004) looked at Jewish communal professionals as a group, noting that some of their findings do not pertain to specific professions. For example, the absence of a career ladder is unlikely to be a reason for a novice day school teacher to leave the field; it is a reason for a campaign associate at a Federation. The CAJE (Coalition for the Advancement of Jewish Education) study (Schaap, 2002) lumps together very part-time professionals, such as synagogue school teachers, with a very small sample of day school teachers. This survey, like the PEN study, asks about the workplace. What keeps these teachers on the job is the compatibility of Jewish education with family life (an issue that I believe is more common among synagogue school teachers than day school teachers and something that certainly motivated Nehama); the compatibility of the profession with living a Jewish life; and satisfaction derived from work (p. 14). This last finding reflects the views of my collaborators. When asked what caused them to consider leaving the field, the CAJE respondents ranked a bad work experience, as did Suzy, Nehama, and Lynn; the need for more money; and the need to receive benefits (p. 15). In her report on retention in Jewish education, Goodman (2002) corroborated that compensation was a significant issue for her respondents. Her findings were not as clear-cut as mine; none of my respondents cited dissatisfaction with salary as the major reason for leaving the field, although both Suzy and Nehama alluded to how ill-paid they were. Goodman's study included novices and veterans, synagogue school teachers, and preschool and day school teachers as one group. Like the PEN and CAJE studies and that of Kelner et al., it surveys professionals currently working in the field, not those who have left.

The study that pertains most directly to mine is the one devised by Johnson and Birkeland (2003). It is longitudinal, deals with novice teachers, and looks at "Leavers," "Movers," and "Stayers." Johnson and Birkeland's Leavers offer a basis for comparison with mine. Their Leavers echo the same kinds of concerns as those of Suzy, Nehama, and Lynn: arbitrary principals (shades of Sylvia Barrett's administrators); inappropriate teaching assignments or materials with no one to help them find their way through them; and the sense of frustration and failure in the classroom. Ranya, a first-year science teacher, sounds very much like

Lynn. Her class seemed to have much diversity, and she had no idea where to get materials to differentiate her instruction. She expected to find, but didn't, students who shared her love of science. To the students, hers was a required class to be endured, not savored. She sought and received little help from the administration. Her story is painfully familiar:

> Ranya believed that skill in engaging and managing a heterogeneous class can be learned, and she hoped that someone at her school would teach her. She had made her needs known early to the administration: "I told them clearly, even before I accepted the job, I said, "I have no experience and I would need some help with this, this, and this." But help was not forthcoming, even when she asked several colleagues for assistance. Ranya's assigned mentor also was responsible for evaluating her, and even as her classroom management problems mounted, she feared that a plea for help would result in a negative evaluation. At the end of her first year, when her contract was not renewed, primarily because of her problems with classroom management, Ranya did not look for a new teaching job. She felt that she had failed as a teacher. She later explained, "I am afraid, at this point, to go out there and fail one more time. I really can't handle that at all." (p. 596)

It is a testimony to Lynn's desire and determination that, feeling as she did about herself as a teacher, she stuck it out as long as she did, reliving her dreadful novice year in two other day school settings. Johnson and Birkeland's Leavers mention other concerns besides feeling ineffectual. They cite issues of autonomy, lack of status, and poor pay; all of them felt inadequately respected and rewarded for their efforts, a prominent theme in my teachers' narratives.

Understanding the Way
That Day Schools Work

Although each of my collaborators left day school teaching, each of the three grew along the continuum of expertise during the course of her time in the field. We have noted earlier that in studying experts in multiple fields, researchers agree that experts perceive more interconnected-

ness, subtlety, and complexity than do novices (Bransford, Brown &
Cocking, 2000; Carter, Cushing, Sabers, Stein & Berliner, 1988;
Copeland, Birmingham, De Meulle, D'Emidio-Caston & Natal, 1994;
Sternberg & Horvath, 1995).

Suzy, Nehama, and Lynn began their preservice experience as graduate students with simplistic notions of day schools based on their
memories as students. Each of them had high hopes for Jewish day
schools as the solution to the problems facing the American Jewish
community. Day schools were powerful places that shaped their Jewish
identity; as teachers in Jewish day schools, they could help instill Jewish
literacy and values in others.

My collaborators saw day schools from a student's perspective. Day
schools were all about what happens in the classroom, in the encounter
between teachers and students. Each of my collaborators emphasized
the dual curriculum, carefully divided between general and Judaic studies, that would be funneled to passive students: *Torah im derekh eretz,*
separate but equal, packaged neatly so that they could be transmitted to
interested students who came from supportive homes. Only Lynn, who
remembered her day school experience most vividly, included cocurricular activities such as field trips, lectures, a Jewish book fair, plays, and a
model seder as opportunities for teaching and learning. As the prospective teachers completed student teaching and entered the world of work,
their understanding became more sophisticated and nuanced. Their perspectives expanded to include boards and administrators who shaped
policy, as well as parents and their financial resources. Suzy and Nehama noted the importance of a school's vision as an impetus for school
decisions and directions.

The literature on teacher growth concludes that more complex understandings of schools and what they do are essential to teacher
growth. But it is difficult to make the case that those complex understandings of school culture help to build a craft. Perceptions cannot
serve as lifeboats for teachers trying to survive. Suzy understood what
her school was trying to accomplish and bought into its vision. But that
perception did not make daily life in the school any easier. Lynn's drawings are full of nervous energy and connectedness. They contain arrows
pointing in every direction and exhibit enormous attention to detail.
Her drawings certainly depict the numerous activities that happen in the
daily routine of day schools; yet Lynn, the talker, and I, her listener/par-
ticipant, were both aware that she was drowning in the details. Each of
my three teachers came to understand that the day school was a com-

munity with diverse interests—those of children, parents, teachers, administrators, and boards; each had to contend with what Deborah Ball (1987) calls the micro-politics of schools. Like Margaret O'Bryan in *The Roller Coaster Year* (Ryan, 1992), who discovered all the "p" words: paperwork, people, programs, and politics (p. 2), all three of my teachers made those discoveries. But more sophisticated perceptions do not guarantee that a teacher will stay in the field.

By the time that these three women were student teachers, they were aware of the complexities of schools. They came to the profession of teaching with what Johnson (1989) calls "embodied knowledge": they had a personal history that included teaching in Jewish schools before. That knowledge shaped their recognition that schools were complex places. Graduate students in Jewish education may be more sophisticated about the micro-politics of schools than their counterparts in general education who have done no teaching when they first enter graduate preparatory programs. While teaching a group of fourteen students getting their master's degrees in education at a secular university, I asked the question, "What worries you most about teaching?" I told them that they could list as many concerns as they chose. I asked the same question to a parallel group studying at the Jewish Theological Seminary in a master's program in Jewish education, which consisted of thirteen students and included Suzy, Nehama, and Lynn. In coding the responses, I found four general categories of concerns: content-knowledge mastery, pedagogical skills, personal attributes, and professional politics.

Concern	General Education Responses	JTS Responses
Lack of content knowledge	6	8
Lack of pedagogical skills	8	8
Lack of personal attributes	3	5
Institutional or professional politics (bureaucracy, colleagues, etc.)	3	7
TOTAL (N=48)	20	28

With 27 respondents, 13 from JTS and 14 from the secular university, I can hardly make any universal statements. But their total of 48 "worries" seems to buttress the findings I derived from talking to Suzy, Lynn, and Nehama and what I read in the novice literature. Both groups were concerned about content knowledge. Would they know enough to teach? Would they be found out as frauds? Would students ask them questions that they couldn't answer? Would the JTS students ever know enough Hebrew? Both groups were concerned about pedagogical skills (8 university; 8 JTS): could they transform the precious metal of knowledge into the coinage of classroom instruction? Could they maintain discipline? Nehama, by her own admission, was terrified by ten-year-olds; Lynn was afraid of turning her back to the class in order to write on the blackboard. Both groups responded similarly to the issue of personal skills. Perhaps the JTS students already know what the general education students suspect: that making a personal connection to one's students is essential.

Preserve students in Jewish education have often had a great deal of experience before entering their professional programs. They have worked, as Suzy, Nehama, and Lynn did, in summer camps, or teaching religious school during college, and while in graduate school. They not only have the apprenticeship of observation that they share with their colleagues in general education, but they have had classrooms of their own, with students to teach, papers to grade, parent-teacher conferences, and relationships with professional colleagues and administrators. They are not really novices to education, although they were novices to day school teaching.

Many students in religious education have been teaching for three, four, or more years before they arrive at the doors of a graduate school. They have been inside schools and know firsthand what all three of my collaborators express after their first year of full-time teaching. In my informal survey of "school worries," seven of the thirteen JTS respondents expressed concerns about the micro-politics of schools. Their professional and personal experiences, prior to entering day school classrooms, have made them aware of the possibility of being caught up in this crossfire. Only three of the university students suspected that institutional politics might trip them up. But, as my teacher talk indicates, knowing that schools must respond to conflicting stakeholders and issues provides no protective armor.

As a researcher, I have to be on the lookout for information that not only corroborates my emerging theory but that also casts doubt upon it. If Suzy, Nehama, and Lynn were aware of the micro-politics of schools from their preservice experiences, why, then, does this personal, practical knowledge not appear on their first concept maps, drawn at approximately the same time that they took my informal survey? I have a hunch that when I asked them to draw their first concept maps, the only day schools that they could imagine were the ones that they had attended. In the survey, which asked an abstract, hypothetical question, they could transfer the knowledge that they had learned while teaching religious school to a future position in the world of day schools. However, the task of imagining a day school evoked context-specific knowledge. In translating it to paper, they reverted to the students they once were and re-created schools from the students' point of view.

Understanding the Role of the Teacher in a Jewish Day School

As Suzy, Nehama, and Lynn gained more experience in teaching Jewish studies, whether in the day school or in the synagogue school, their perceptions of the teachers' roles changed. Their original concept maps, drawn when they were preservice teachers, included two walled-off areas, one labeled "general studies," and the second labeled "Jewish studies." As preservice teachers, they assumed that they would stay behind those walls. Being able to stay within the lines proved to be impossible. By the time that Lynn had completed student teaching, she had noticed the balancing act that day school teachers do: trading time with their secular studies counterparts. Nehama, who did her student teaching with Rina, the special-projects coordinator, learned early on about the extension of curriculum into cocurricular activities. Suzy, who taught in a school that prided itself on its integrated approach toward Jewish and general studies, had her heart set on teaching in that kind of school; it was a reaction to teaching in a day school with rigid demarcations. Her comment about the unheralded power of a secular teacher to influence children's values is an indicator of her realization of what Lynn calls "balance": the sharing of time, space, and power.

None of the three anticipated how much time she would have to spend with another aspect of balance: that is, dealing with the needs of her students vis-à-vis the needs of the curriculum. Josh, the encopretic student, highlighted the tension for Suzy; caring about her students preceded caring about the curriculum. Nehama expressed her priorities in shelving the teaching of *Mah Nishtanah* (the Four Questions) for her students' comfort and wandering attention. The diversity of her students drained Lynn, who knew intellectually that she had to meet their needs but was at her wits' end as to how to do so. She recalled her feelings of being unable to balance the expectation of being attentive to each of her students with that of being an instructional leader, preparing her students to meet the curricular expectations of the group.

> [I remember] being overwhelmed by the diversity of the students I had to teach, trying to balance a lesson for an Israeli, plus a sort of middle-ground American who grew up Russian and who had only been here a year or two. I also had a couple of kids who are both LD and ADHD, and one of them was from a severely troubled home so I was really struggling all year trying to figure out what to do with this kid. How do I keep him as part of my class but so that he feels like he's getting something? *(interview, 1999)*

As the three became involved in Jewish education, each articulated her concerns for moral education. Nehama saw the school as an antidote for "sex, drugs, and rock and roll." Suzy was insistent on the school's need to provide a community of caring. Lynn was hoping to inculcate a sense of restraint and respect in her students to counteract the rudeness that had never been dealt with by their parents. Whether they talked about caring or control, each expressed the belief that moral education was part of her job description.

As I compare the students I met as preservice day school teachers with those I taught preparing to become teachers in public education, I am convinced that a religious or spiritual bent predisposes a teacher to moral education. There is no need to "sell" them on the place of moral education in their teaching. This is not the exclusive purview of religious educators; these qualities can be found within general educators as well. In another study on moral education in middle schools, I sought out teachers who took moral education seriously in their teaching. I relied on the opinion of what Eisner calls "connoisseurs." I studied four educators in different communities, teaching different subject matters. Only one was a religious educator by definition. But all four, whether they taught Bible, math, American history, or English, were people for whom religion and spirituality were essential (Ingall, 1997). David Hansen's *The Call to Teach* (1995) discovered a similar phenomenon. Jewish day school teachers share a great deal with teachers predisposed to religion and spirituality in other settings.

Although teaching is a calling for most teachers, there is an added intensity to the vocation of religious educator. The differences lie in the nature of the field and one's induction into the field. A literature teacher may stumble upon the realization that teaching the moral issues in *To Kill a Mockingbird* is as important as looking for literary devices, but for religious educators, it's all about moral education. Teachers in religious institutions are expected to be role models—what Suzy referred to as *dugmaot*. Their job is to enculturate their students, as Lynn and Nehama discovered, into a tradition that may not always seem relevant to their students. If they don't make connections to their students' lives, they fail. The Jewish communal obsession with loss makes the stakes even higher in Jewish education than in other religious traditions.

As their portraitist, I have to consider the context, or the background, of my subjects. I have discussed their personal contexts and their family, educational, and religious backgrounds. Part of the context is also historical and sociological. They entered graduate school during the height of the "continuity campaigns" unleashed in the aftermath of the 1990–91 National Jewish Population Study. Each of my collaborators believed that her profession was essential to the survival of the Jewish community. The hype on Jewish day schools was at an all-time high. Suzy, Nehama, and Lynn were intending to save Jewish souls. Their failure still hurts, years later.

Changes over Time

According to Feiman-Nemser (1983), research on how teachers learn to teach is very spotty. It is sparser still in the world of religious education. One of the outcomes of my research, ten years of teacher talk, is a body of data that represents reflections by novices over time on their teacher preparation, student teaching, and socialization into the profession of day school teaching. In addition, the data include those reflections that fall into the category of Johnson's embodied knowledge, the years of pretraining influences (Feiman-Nemser, 1983), which include the "apprenticeship of observation"—for example, the years that Suzy, Nehama, and Lynn spent as students and campers. Other pretraining influences might include attitudes that they absorbed at home, as children of parents involved professionally or avocationally in education and Jewish day schools. Other influences are reflections on the time they spent as college and graduate students, defraying the high cost of tuition by moonlighting as part-time teachers in religious schools. Feiman-Nemser (1983) reminds her readers of "the pervasive effects of these formative experiences" (p. 152). As we have seen from their first concept maps, it is from the pretraining aspects of their lives that novices develop attitudes, dispositions, and preconceptions about teaching.

Some of my teachers' preconceptions changed very little over time. Their tacit assumptions (Elbaz, 1991) remained remarkably constant. All three demonstrated the robustness of their personal and professional biographies, their "embodied knowledge" (Johnson, 1989) or "implicit theories" (Clark & Yinger, 1977). Suzy never wavered on the need for schools to be sanctuaries and the role of teachers as moral educators. Lynn never changed her vision of teaching as being a Jewish culture bearer while searching for that elusive "stage presence." Nehama, the least ideological and most pragmatic of the three, responded to adversity by quoting, "Man plans, and God laughs" and carried an umbrella in case of rain.

What did change was the knowledge that could be learned only through experience. I referred above to a change that has been documented in the literature of novice teachers, the growing understanding that schools are complex institutions. As Knowles (1988) aptly describes the process, young teachers lose their "nearsightedness." Nehama's understanding that the unsung heroes of school life were the school secretary and custodian is a "farsighted" realization that could emerge only through experience. A second example is Suzy's awareness that teachers might plan a perfect lesson on paper that could fail because of an unpredictable student confrontation over lunch. Their expanding awareness of the micro-politics of schools, gained in the field, made all three teachers more sensitive to school bureaucracy, procedures, and parent-school relationships.

A second change, also derived from experience, dealt with what teacher educators refer to as "situated learning." Each of my three collaborators learned how context-specific teaching is. Lynn realized that another teacher's formulas for success might not work for her. The Orthodox *rebbetzin* could command the attention of her students because she saw them both in and out of school. Suzy discovered that two kindergarten classes could be very different. Nehama observed that a veteran teacher worked very differently with one colleague from the way she worked with another.

Each of the three moved along the continuum from novice to expert, in different domains and in different degrees. Their progress and their professional growth make their leaving the field that much sadder. I have suggested earlier that, unlike Wadsworth's (2001) teachers who stayed, my collaborators found that teaching had ceased to be fun. But there is more. Reviewing the transcripts of their interviews, looking over their correspondence and concept maps, I am struck by a change in attitude over time: a gradual erosion of the idealism that brought them into the field in the first place. Sylvia Barrett's idealism was renewed; my teachers' idealism went unrewarded.

Each of the three approached day school teaching with high hopes of finding students like themselves, of being a part of a venture of enormous import, of making a contribution to the American Jewish community. Each felt that the Jewish day school was *sui generis,* very different from the synagogue school that met for fewer hours and that was always a poor competitor for the attention of students and parents, far down a list that included more compelling alternatives, such as ballet and soccer. Both Nehama and Lynn were dejected to discover that Judaic studies was a stepchild to general studies, an observation made by other day school teachers as well. Irit Goldstein, a Judaic studies teacher in a Jewish day high school, learned it as well (Ingall & Malkus, 2001). Irit tried to enhance the place of Judaic studies in the life of the school through transdisciplinary programs, linking Jewish philosophy and art, or American history and Jewish history. Suzy began her "induction phase of learning to teach" (Feiman-Nemser, 1983) with a commitment to curricular integration; Nehama and Lynn flirted with its possibilities over time. Perhaps their thoughts about integration evolved through experience as they recognized the permeable boundaries between the dual curriculum in day schools. What Lynn called "balance" was a factor of daily life. One way to maintain balance, to even off the tradeoffs of time, personnel, and space, was to create programs that bridge the demarcations of the Judaic and secular. But without a full-blown commitment to integration, the reminders of a lesser status accorded to Jewish learning were all too painful.

Suzy, teaching in a school that from its very inception ascribed to a curricular philosophy of transdisciplinary integration, did not experience the second-class status of Judaic studies. However, her idealism, like that of the others, was shattered. Just as Nehama and Lynn had to question their commitment to passing Jewish learning on in schools that scheduled play rehearsals during *Humash* time (Nehama) or to children from families who were indifferent to Hebrew and observance (Lynn), Suzy began to question her role as a day school teacher. When she butted heads with the administration about the social and emotional needs of the children in her care, she wondered what being a teacher really meant. All three of my respondents struggled to survive as inexperienced teachers without much support from administrators and colleagues. In addition, their deep-seated personal knowledge about teaching and learning was assailed. Teaching in a day school was not as they had imagined it. This was the coup de grace that enervated them far more than the demands of lesson planning, creating curricula, and dealing with difficult children and parents. Lynn looked in vain for students like herself; Nehama missed passing her heritage on as part of a well-functioning team; Suzy was committed to a vision of teaching as caring—a vision that, to her supervisor, looked more like social work than teaching. For each, the loss of her idealism was the factor that tipped the balance. To work as hard as they were working, to struggle to survive, and, at the end of a long day, to question the entity to which they were devoting this energy: all this was too high a price to pay. All three of them became physically and spiritually ill. To paraphrase Parker Palmer (1998–99), they became teachers for reasons of the heart and lost heart as time went by. Unlike Sylvia Barrett, who resumed teaching after her broken leg healed, Suzy, Nehama, and Lynn left the ranks of day school teachers, heartbroken.

CHAPTER SIX

Implications for the Field

Qualitative research in education, if done with art and rigor, provides the reader with deeply etched depictions of small-scale truths. Readers hungering for grand landscapes should look for them elsewhere. This methodology asks them to be satisfied with cameos bearing no certificates of universality—only limited promises of authenticity. However, limitations can prove to be strengths. As Louis Menand (2001) reassures his readers, skepticism (and, I would add, modesty as well) can be the ally of inquiry: "The greater our awareness of the fallibility of our understanding and the provisional nature of our concepts, the more techniques we devise for perfecting our data and the more pains we take to verify our conclusions" (p. 80). While working with my three collaborators over ten years, relying on multiple sources such as interviews, concept maps, and artifactual data, I have tried to build in mechanisms to ensure validity. By sharing my observations with Suzy, Nehama, and Lynn, by encouraging them to add or subtract from my narratives, I have added another layer of honesty to the account. Would another researcher come to the same conclusions? I don't know. In portraiture, such a question is irrelevant. A portrait of King David created by Rembrandt most assuredly differs from one painted by Chagall or Caravaggio. Do the differences make any one of the three portraits less true? Might each portrait enrich our understanding of the essence of King David?

What I have tried to do is to capture the thought processes of Suzy, Nehama, and Lynn over time and come to some conclusions about their attitudes based on themes that recurred in their teacher talk, their writing, and their concept maps. Might the narratives be different had I worked with a different set of teachers? Might the narratives be different had Suzy, Nehama, and Lynn spoken with a different researcher? Might the narratives be different if they were not occurring in a period when people changed jobs frequently? When day schools were being touted as the salvation of the American Jewish community and bursting into bloom across the Jewish communal landscape? Possibly. But by collecting the data over time and by examining recurring patterns in the various data sources, I have isolated themes that remain significant for each of the teachers and among the three teachers. The patterns and the rich detail from which they are derived avoid the tyranny of abstraction and invest the portraits and my conclusions with what Bruner (1986) refers to as "verisimilitude."

Education is a field that is deeply embedded in the world of practice and, as such, is hungry for answers to the complex questions that arise from the classroom. Practitioners are dissatisfied with tiny morsels of truth, no matter how tasty, particularly in a field like Jewish day school education, with a relatively sparse research literature and such high stakes. While it is tempting to hide behind my cameos, begging the question of generalizability, I am obliged to tease out some lessons for the field. Anne Fausto-Sterling (1985) encourages researchers "to articulate, both to themselves and publicly, exactly where they stand, what they think and most importantly, what they feel deep down in their guts about the complex of personal and social issues that relate to their area of research" (p. 10). I will try to satiate some of that hunger with suggestions, based on what I learned from my collaborators' conversations, for the audience that is most likely to read this book: teacher educators, day school administrators, and funders and policymakers.

For Teacher Educators

While doing the research for this book, I have been involved in teaching prospective day school teachers. My study served as a form of action research, offering me insights into my own teaching, not only that of my collaborators. While I was gathering and interpreting data, I changed the way that I taught the practicum in day school education. When I first began to teach the course—the same year that Suzy, Nehama, and Lynn began their studies—the practicum consisted of one semester of student teaching in the field, together with a seminar designed to reflect upon that practice. Since our students were still completing course work in both Judaic studies and in Jewish education, the student teaching experience was left to the last semester of their last year in a master's program. Students spent two days a week in the field, while finishing up requirements, writing a master's thesis, and often—because it was held during the second semester—trying to find jobs. Each class had one or two students planning weddings or anticipating the arrival of new babies. (Needless to say, the bulk of our students are women, a theme I will return to later.) Our students entered the field in January, feeling overwhelmed by the large shadow of graduation. In addition, they entered a classroom *in medias res*. Not being a part of the process in September, they were unaware of how a teacher socialized her students into the mores of her classroom and the norms of the school. By the time they were oriented into the life of the school, it was Passover, and graduation was around the corner.

One of the first changes I made was to extend the seminar to a full year and to encourage our students, along with their cooperating teachers, to attend the preschool orientation programs. Another was to persuade as many students as I could to amortize the degree over three years instead of two. That way, they could do the course work over two years and save their student teaching and master's project for the third. By introducing an internship during the second year, during which time they would observe in a day school and serve as unpaid student assistants, they could acquire a feel for the culture of the school and an opportunity to learn whether this setting was one in which they might be professionally comfortable. The internship also allowed the administration to get to know our student and to see if he or she might fit in well as a paid member of the faculty. If there was a good match, the student could be hired as a new part-time teacher, with provisions made, if necessary, to complete remaining course work, or as a full-time faculty member who would be excused from after-school responsibilities to attend the seminar at the Jewish Theological Seminary. Like our student teachers, these part-time hires received supervision as a component of the practicum.

We have begun to introduce all our students, not only those in the day school concentration, to supervision in their first year. All our students take a Skills for Teaching class; in order to take it, they must be engaged in teaching in a Jewish educational venue. This part-time teaching affords them a laboratory in which to practice and a site for supervision. Each student is paired with a senior practitioner or advanced doctoral student who provides a listening ear and a skilled eye, introducing the student to supervision that is not tied to evaluation and a renewal of a contract.

Ideally, I would like to have all our students complete their course work before undergoing a year in the field, with staggered entry during their pre-practicum years. If all students were able to undergo an internship each year, in different venues (community schools and denominational schools; elementary and secondary schools; schools with integrated curricula and traditional binary programs; schools in the city and schools in the suburbs), their education would be enriched immeasurably. This was a suggestion that Lynn made as well, noting that had she served as an intern in an elementary school, she would not have chosen to do her practicum in a middle school.

I would also recommend that we teacher educators respond to my collaborators' realization that religious education is inseparable from moral education. In the best of worlds, preservice Jewish day school teachers should take a course in moral education. If that is impossible, then the discussion of moral education ought to be woven into the fabric of the curriculum as part of their methods courses or as a part of their student teaching.

Undertaking this research has convinced me of the robustness of the teachers' pretraining experience, an issue discussed in the literature of novice teachers (Feiman-Nemser, 1983). The fact that each of these graduate students drew a concept map of a day school from a student's point of view is compelling proof that prospective teachers don't begin to think like teachers just because they have declared their intention to become teachers. This understanding has made me rethink the content of my practicum and has convinced me to deal with personal, practical knowledge explicitly. I now begin the seminar by eliciting student memories of day school education (in the case of students who are themselves the products of day schools) or impressions of Jewish day schools for those students who did not attend these institutions. I try to use those impressions as a touchstone to which we periodically return throughout the course of the year.

I am also convinced that we are doing the students a disservice by not factoring in their collegiate and graduate experiences as teachers in synagogue and religious schools. By ignoring this experience, we overlook a rich source of experience that can be compared with what our students encounter during their student teaching in day schools. By asking them to contrast these two arenas of Jewish education, we not only sharpen their powers of observation, but we encourage our students to treat these part-time jobs more professionally. Rather than merely being an alternative to waiting on tables, teaching in a religious school is another opportunity in which to gain classroom skills, practice assessment, and deal with parents, administrators, and colleagues—all of which translates into teaching in a day school.

As a teacher educator, I have set great store in reflective practice, carving out numerous opportunities in my seminar for students to think through issues of curriculum and instruction. They keep journals, read and write cases, and produce portfolios of their work along with soul-searching narratives about their philosophy and pedagogy. While I am not ready to jump aboard the postmodernist bandwagon and claim that reason isn't what it's cracked up to be, I am somewhat guarded about its long-term benefits. Lynn's struggle, as documented both in her interviews and in her concept maps, is a stirring reminder that understanding does not always lead to action. Lynn quickly lost what Knowles (1988) calls her "near-sightedness"; but seeing "the big picture" with all its complexity did not liberate her. The detail became overwhelming, if not downright paralyzing. While still convinced of the need to encourage reflection in practice, I now spend more time on videotaping students as they teach and using the videotapes to discuss the context-specific nature of their practice.

Another strategy to beef up the preservice experience of our students is one that we are just beginning to explore: creating stronger partnerships with the field by establishing professional development schools. Reimer (cited in *Agenda*, 2004) agrees: "It's not so far-fetched to imagine that our master teachers might on some level participate as clinical professors in graduate programs of Jewish education" (p. 7). Heller (2004) summarizes the benefits of a truly reciprocal relationship between the academy and the field. These benefits include better training for the student teacher and cooperating teachers; enhancing the status of the cooperating teacher by making him or her an equal partner alongside the university professor; and affording the possibility of ongoing professional development for the school faculties (p. 27).

Feiman-Nemser (1983) suggests that we teacher educators think of teacher induction as a four-stage process: pretraining; preservice experience; the first year, which she calls "induction"; and in-service over the teacher's career (p. 151). In this section, I have tried to deal with the first two of Feiman-Nemser's phases, what teacher educators can accomplish prior to the entrance of the novice teacher into the world of work. They can help the fledgling teacher learn to reflect upon his or her own understanding of Jewish education, its vision and practice, and recollections or perceptions of Jewish day schools. Teacher educators can help reinforce habits of mind; they can introduce students to the culture of day schools; they can give them a glimpse of what to aspire to, that is, the sophisticated perception that characterizes experts; and finally—perhaps the most important understanding—they can encourage students to think of the problems that they face in student teaching as learning opportunities.

But the real learning must take place in a classroom where new teachers are flying solo, with students of their own, and without the presence of a cooperating teacher to help them muddle through. Because schooling is so context-specific, it is impossible to anticipate all the problems that these young teachers will meet in the field. Professional skills simply cannot be front-end-loaded during preservice education. I have referred to the work of Bransford et al. (2000) earlier. That process of "noticing the accidents"* can only happen in the field. Therefore the burden of helping new teachers acquire practical professional knowledge lies with the administration.

Fable (For Herbert Kohl)

Yes it was the prince's kiss.
But the way was prepared for the prince.
It had to be.
When the attendants carrying the woman
—dead they thought her lying on the litter—
stumbled over the root of a tree
the bit of deathly apple in her throat
jolted free.
Not strangled, not poisoned!
She
can come alive.
It was an "accident" they hardly noticed.
The threshold here comes when they stumble.
The jolt. And better if we notice.
However, their noticing is not
Essential to the story.
A miracle has even deeper roots,
Something like error, some profound defeat.
Stumbled over, the startle, the arousal,
Something never perceived till now, the taproot.

---

* The poet Muriel Rukeyser dedicated her poem "Fable" to the progressive educator Herbert Kohl, her good friend (cited in H. Kohl [1998], pp. 128–29).

For Day School Administrators

All three teachers who participated in this research experienced a wretched first year and lack of support by their administrators. Suzy had turned to members of the school administration on numerous occasions regarding her first co-teacher. The message that she received was to work it out for herself. Nehama kept hoping for some sort of intervention from a supervisor to alleviate the discomfort she felt in her team-teaching situation. Although she was the "junior partner" and could not leapfrog over the more seasoned members of the team, she knew that at least one of her co-teachers was discussing the situation with the administration. Not only did the administrators fail to meet with the team to sort through the issues that had arisen, but they also kept the same unhappy team in place for a second miserable year. Lynn was hungry for help, finally receiving it in her second and third schools. But Lynn's perception was that this support was either not enough or not very helpful. As she recalled the most recent mentoring that she received, it usually consisted of sitting in on another teacher's class and observing how she dealt with class management issues. But what Lynn sought was context-specific, not generic; she wanted coaching to resolve issues that emerged from her classroom, not from another's. As she tried to maintain order, her commitment to creative teaching waned. Like Molly Ness (2001), who reflects on her first year of teaching with Teach for America, Lynn was "becoming the worksheet teacher that [she] swore [she] would never be" (p. 701). Frustration and failure bred further frustration and failure. In the case of each of my collaborators, the heads of their schools were in survival mode themselves; they had little time for the struggles of their new teachers. Zmuda, Kuklis, and Kline (2004), quoting Senge, describe administrators much as I have described Lynn, as "drowning in events" (p. 33).

The Voice of the New Teacher (Public Education Network, 2003) puts the onus of responsibility for retaining new teachers on the administration. Administrators, no matter how preoccupied they may be putting out fires, simply have to make enculturating and teaching new teachers a priority. "Principals can make or break a new teacher. New teachers working in schools run by principals they describe as effective and competent had a much easier transition into teaching" (p. 24). One of the strategies that effective principals use is mentoring.

Mentoring

The literature of general education has much to tell us about why teachers leave the field. This literature reminds us that young teachers and seasoned teachers leave teaching for different reasons. Tye and O'Brien (2002) make this age distinction when they review the literature, which consistently notes "a bimodal curve: most of those who leave teaching in any given year are either *disillusioned beginners with just two or three years in the classroom* or 30-year veterans who are ready to retire" (p. 25; italics mine) and then proceed to study why the experienced teachers leave teaching. My collaborators all fall into the "disillusioned beginner" category, teachers who do not mention top-down curriculum, paperwork, or the shadow of standardized testing. For them, the lack of mentoring was a *cri de coeur* that resonated throughout their narratives.

Day school teaching must be thought of as a craft as much as a profession. Crafts are learned through apprenticeships, through mentoring. In a recent conversation, a glassblower whose work I had admired told me that newcomers arrive in her studio having learned the theory elsewhere; they come to her to learn technique. In the studio, their entry into this ancient guild is carefully supervised through the parceling out of discrete tasks by master craftspersons. Mentors can serve this role in day schools. They are crucial in providing support and helping a newcomer become socialized into the life of the school. My collaborators, like so many others, were left to figure things out for themselves, or to fail to figure things out for themselves, without mentors in the field.

In her article "What New Teachers Need to Learn," Feiman-Nemser (2003) delineates some of the outcomes for which a mentor would be helpful: picking up pedagogical content knowledge, or what she calls "situationally relevant approaches to subject matter"; crafting a teacher persona; dealing with day-to-day classroom concerns such as transitions and management; reading classroom "signs" and responding to them "on their feet"; and figuring out school culture (pp. 26–27). Kilbourn and Roberts (1991) capture the interactions between a first-year teacher, May, and her mentor, Steve. These conversations deal with the essentials of teaching and learning: the affective as well as the cognitive dimensions of teaching; power and powerlessness; and balancing the needs of the teacher with those of the learners.

While mentors can provide support, encouragement, and a friendly ear, they should also push their mentees. Vygotsky's dictum comes to mind: maximum support and maximum challenge. The role of the mentor should be to structure the educative experiences that help the preservice teacher acquire what she needs to know. Feiman-Nemser (2001) refers to this process as "educative mentoring." An experienced school administrator like Heller (2004, p. 37) posits an agenda for educative mentoring. His to-do list for mentors includes teaching the following:

- The "nuts and bolts" of the system
- Lesson planning
- Methodology
- Parent conferences
- Classroom management

Induction Programs

Assigning a novice teacher a mentor is just a beginning. Inducting a new teacher into the profession is a multilayered experience that must first be conceptualized and then implemented by the school administration. It must begin with a holistic conception of what induction means. Cheryl Finkel, a seasoned day school principal, suggests that administrators consider their new hires as preservice teachers and structure learning experiences for them to fill in the gaps in their education:

> I think those of us who don't live in Boston and New York have certainly hired Jewish studies teachers who have necessitated "taking down barriers." They may be teachers or they may be Hebrew speakers or may be Judaically knowledgeable but not Hebrew speakers. They are often people whom we consider having big gaps, but we take them in and we try to take the place of a university and train them on the job in Jewish practice and Jewish commitment, and we try to excite them and create a new sense of Jewish identity, in some cases, depending on which gap we are trying to address. (*Agenda*, 2004, pp. 4–5)

Feiman-Nemser (2003) reminds us that administrators tend to think of their new hires as finished products when they are, in fact, works in progress. She, like Finkel, insists that administrators think differently about their new hires. An induction program must begin with the assumption that teachers are still learners, an assumption that characterizes the medical profession with a much longer staged entry into the profession.

In addition to thinking about the first years of teaching as an extension of the preservice experience, induction also means that an administrator must structure a web of experiences for the novice, not merely assign her to a well-meaning veteran with no discussion of expectations and outcomes. The literature on induction suggests that teachers as well as administrators find that the most efficacious forms of professional development for new teachers are multidimensional and interactive (Perez, Swain & Hartsough, 1997). Interactive practices include mentoring, lesson observation, conferencing, coaching, and teaming, all of which are designed to give long-term support for new teachers.

The most comprehensive study of teacher induction programs that I have found is Curran and Goldrick's (2002) brief for the National Governors' Association. They learned that what characterizes the most thoughtful induction programs are an orientation to the culture of teaching; training in curriculum and management skills; mentoring; and assessments and feedback to gauge the learning of the novices (p. 4). In the best programs, all the new teachers were required to participate; experienced and trained mentors were involved; both parties—the mentors and the novices—were given released time for their work; there were funds earmarked for the program; clear standards were set; the program was designed collaboratively with the help of the novices and the mentors; the performance of the novices was regularly assessed; the "educative mentoring" had a subject-specific focus; and rather than thinking of induction as a first-year activity—as Feiman-Nemser (2003) does—they recommend an extension of the induction period to subsequent years of teaching (Curran & Goldrick, p. 5). Such sophisticated, holistic induction programs require a school administrator to make teacher retention, as well as recruitment, a priority.

Creating a Learning Community

Peerless (2002) astutely observes that mentoring (and, by extension, any teacher induction program) is a countercultural enterprise in most schools. Teachers teach behind high walls in their "egg-carton" classrooms. Working in teams or participating in peer observation is foreign to them. The norm is solo practitioners, working autonomously. One exciting outcome of a thoughtful induction process is that it can help to change the culture of a day school, making peer coaching, reflective teaching, and learning (mentors must be trained, after all) a norm in the school. When teacher induction is implemented on a larger scale, Peerless believes that it can change the entire staff (p. 67). Zmuda et al. (2004) suggest that the way new teachers are cultivated can foreshadow a seismic change in school culture: from individual autonomy to collective autonomy. Senge (Smith, 2001) defines a learning organization as a place "where people continually expand their capacity to create the results they truly desire, where new and expansive patterns of thinking are nurtured, where collective aspiration is set free, and where people are continually learning to see the whole together." There are few such learning organizations studding the Jewish day school landscape. True learning organizations foster the personal and professional satisfaction that Suzy, Nehama, and Lynn found lacking. As Williams (2003) discovered in her study of teachers who stay in teaching, the ups and downs of the job and the pressure to teach well no matter how taxing the challenges demand the support of a community and an appreciative administration. Learning communities know how to balance the loss of personal resources with opportunities to renew them.

Nourishing the Personal and the Professional

Ness (2001) points to an aspect of teaching that must be recognized by day school administrators. Schools must serve teachers' personal needs as well as the psychological needs of students. One's personhood is tied up in one's profession. Lynn's problems in the classroom made her feel like a personal, as well as a professional, failure. Nehama deliberately chose not to be a public school teacher. She wanted to teach in a day school in order to live by the same school calendar as her family (to "march to the beat of the Jewish calendar," as Suzy once described day school teaching). Suzy wanted to be surrounded by a Jewish community, a welcome change from her early years of living in the South. Being told that her outreach to a troubled child's mother was too "social-worky" was an attack not only on her notion of what teaching was all about, but also on who she was.

   Pomson (2001) urges administrators to be cognizant of the fact that Jewish schools are vehicles of meaning not only for students but for teachers as well. This is another way of framing the lesson learned by Wadsworth (2001) in her research with veteran teachers: teachers will put up with minimal pay as long as there are psychological rewards. When those rewards wane, vocation is not enough. Suzy reviews some of those rewards, all of which are situated at the crossroads of the personal and professional:

The day school, as an institution, has enormous potential for impact on a child's Jewish identity. *But many factors must be in place for the environment to be rewarding for everyone.* The teachers need support, the children need teachers who are supportive and well-trained, and every school must be mindful of the varying needs of all its populations. Needs include those psychological (support for issues that children are dealing with and multiple administrators for teachers to utilize) and financial (teachers need to be compensated especially for the work they do that extends beyond the school day: family education, writing Purim spiels, etc.). I could go on and on. . . . *In essence, it's haval [regrettable] that the intrinsic rewards of being a Jewish educator, after several years with the best of intentions, but the "wrong" environment, aren't enough to retain even the ones who "really care."* I feel a bit like Rodney Dangerfield for saying this, but as a day school teacher, "I didn't get no respect!" Or, shall I say, not enough to keep me there. (personal communication, August 27, 2001; italics mine)

Patricia Houghton (2001) offers some suggestions for administrators to nourish teachers' personal needs. Houghton quotes Deborah Meier, founder of the Central Park East Schools in Harlem and the creative force behind other charter school initiatives, who urges administrators to help teachers renew their commitment to teaching through their choice of allies. Allies break down teacher isolation and promote psychological well-being. They can be found in schools that promote teacher community, in professional groups and conferences, in professional literature, and in pursuing further education. Sympathetic colleagues help teachers "to be mindful of all that is beautiful and glorious about being a teacher" (p. 711).

For Funders and Policymakers

My research suggests some implications for retaining day school teachers that are simply too expensive or sweeping for individual schools to initiate on their own. I suggest below some initiatives for consideration by those interested in making change on a more systemic scale.

Outstanding Professional Education Opportunities

In studying veteran teachers, Williams (2003) learned that the most powerful professional renewal opportunities were ones that afforded them intense learning experiences and reflection, such as sabbaticals and weeklong retreats (p. 74). It is unlikely that Jewish day schools struggling to meet their payrolls, led by floundering administrators, will be able to provide comprehensive programs for the professional and personal nurture that young day school teachers need in order to survive and to become veteran teachers like those Williams interviewed. Decades ago, the Melton Research Center realized the need for teacher retreats to feed the mind and the spirit. These retreats were simply too expensive for the center to maintain. It is time to reconsider them.

The Avi Chai Foundation funded its first *Ivriyon* during the summer of 2004. Day school teachers with three to five years of experience met at the Jewish Theological Seminary for a five-week Hebrew immersion program designed for Judaica teachers in grades three through eight. Although there have been no published evaluation studies of the program, I have heard from my former students how welcome (and grueling) the *Ivriyon* was. Hebrew language instruction, learning pedagogical content knowledge across the curriculum (e.g., in prayer, *Tanakh,* as well as Hebrew language instruction), and recreational activities combined to build confidence and energize those teachers who were en route to becoming expert teachers.

Sabbaticals are generally too expensive for day schools to consider. Even if they were affordable, administrators would probably claim that a cadre of teacher substitutes to replace those on leave simply does not exist. One wonders if the exodus of seasoned educators from day schools to public schools (an exodus that affects even those teachers and administrators with backgrounds in Jewish education) might be stanched with the introduction of sabbaticals. There are now several prizes funded by family foundations for outstanding Jewish teachers. Imagine the existence of a fund that would pay for a semester sabbatical for talented Jewish day school educators.

Salary Increases

In a special issue of *Jewish Education News* on *kavod* and teacher retention, Roberta Louis Goodman (2002) makes the claim that pumping up salaries might solve teacher attrition in Jewish schools. She lumps together Judaic and general studies teachers, which somewhat muddies her conclusions, but her findings deserve further study. Goodman notes that for over two-thirds of the teachers—consisting of Judaic as well as secular studies teachers—the leading response to the question "Why might you leave the field?" was the need for increased income (p. 26). Although my collaborators did not point to low salaries as being the primary reason for their leaving the field, Suzy certainly mentioned her low salary in one of our more recent interviews. Noting that she was now well remunerated in her communal position, she acknowledged that she would have been more willing to put up with the unsupportive school administration and poor working conditions had she been better paid. Nehama commented that she was reasonably compensated for teaching in a synagogue school. Her hourly rate, for instruction, which required limited planning, was far higher than what it was as a day school teacher.

The salary issue is causing a "blackboard brain drain" in general education, a factor that is crucial in a field competing now with medicine, law, and engineering for talented women applicants (O'Donnell, 2004). O'Donnell, citing economics professor Caroline Hoxby, notes an anomaly in the teaching profession: high-performing teachers earn no more than their counterparts who perform poorly (p. 19). The brightest teachers are most likely to leave (Heller, 2004, p. 5), and there are fewer outstanding candidates to replace them. In Jewish education, the day school faces competition from other arenas of Jewish education. There is much more money to be made as a synagogue school administrator or in working for philanthropic foundations with education portfolios.

Suzy, Nehama, and Lynn were part of a cohort of twelve preservice day school teachers, ten women and two men, during their last year of graduate school. The men, both rabbis, have become administrators and remain in the field. Of the ten women in the group, only four are still teaching in day schools. None have become administrators in day schools. The sample is far too small to provide any conclusions, but it does suggest that the women, receiving far lower salaries than their male counterparts in day schools and lower salaries than synagogue school principals, were likely to vote with their feet. The issues of gender and attrition, of gender and salary, and the impact of rabbis as teacher/administrators on the day school teacher pool bear further study.

Underwriting some of the salaries of Jewish day school teachers cannot come from the schools themselves. Neither can the initiative come from Federations struggling with flat campaigns and an ideological reluctance to support denominational schools. Federations might be persuaded to provide more support for higher salaries of teachers in community schools; family foundations might be ready to fund higher salaries of Jewish day teachers in denominational schools. While skeptics claim that we can't solve every problem by throwing money in its direction, the data suggest that teacher retention is one that might be cured with the application of a greenback poultice.

Creating the Career Ladder

During the ten years I have spent researching and writing this study, there has been a flurry of new day school teacher initiatives funded by the successors to the traditional Hebrew teachers' colleges, or launched on the campuses of secular universities, or brokered by private philanthropies. (At least two of the latter have fizzled out over this period.) While all of us involved in day school education laud these efforts, my research has convinced me that just as much attention must be paid to retention as to recruitment. Although the two are often linked rhetorically as a single issue, far more attention and ink are spent on recruitment. In fact, there are few examples of in-depth research on retention. The inaugural issue of the e-newsletter of JERRI (2004), the Jewish Education Recruitment and Retention Initiative, jointly sponsored by JESNA and the Covenant Foundation, featured three stories on bringing new teachers into the field and nothing whatsoever on retention.

Ingersoll, the dean of the teacher attrition researchers, calls recruitment "the wrong solution to the teacher shortage" (Ingersoll and Smith, 2003). About one-quarter of new teachers leave the profession within the first three years of teaching, and 30 percent leave within the first five years of teaching (Curran & Goldrick, 2002). If it does take five to eight years to learn the craft, as Berliner suggests (Scherer, 2001), it is a colossal waste of precious Jewish communal funds to identify newcomers to teaching, educate them, and then lose them to other professions. Smith and Ingersoll (2004) state unequivocally that the problem of general education is not a teacher shortage: "[S]chool staffing problems are to a large extent the result of a 'revolving door': Large numbers of teachers leave teaching jobs long before retirement" (p. 682). Jewish educators perennially wring their hands over "the personnel crisis," by which they mean the teacher shortage. In fact, the more serious issue is that of teacher attrition and the shortage of trained mentors to break down the revolving door.

There are national programs to prepare new principals for synagogue schools. Perhaps this is the right time for a centrally based program for new day school teachers. There are models for such programs in the world of general education. Arizona State University, under David Berliner's leadership, provides mentoring for more than a thousand teachers in their first two years of teaching. As Berliner notes, the program, using university and school-based supervisors, costs but a few hundred dollars per teacher per year, cutting dropout losses significantly (Scherer, 2001).

Just as funds are available for cultivating day school leaders (the Avi Chai Foundation has been funding cohorts of educational leaders in a program implemented by the Davidson Graduate School of Jewish Education), funds must also be made available on a national level for training mentors and master teachers for novices. The Mandel Foundation's Teacher Education Initiative (TEI), a national program designed to improve professional development for Jewish educators, might serve as a model. An infusion of philanthropic funds to create such partnerships for Jewish day schools would help to keep the future Suzys, Nehamas, and Lynns in the profession.

In addition to adding to the clinical staff of Jewish teacher education programs, such a program would also create a new tier of professional teacher educators—master teachers or mentors—in the day schools. The call for building a career ladder in general education once reverberated in the reform literature of the 1980s (Carnegie Forum on Education and the Economy, 1986; The Holmes Group, 1986). A career ladder creates new opportunities for the profession, adding to the two rungs labeled "classroom teacher" or "administrator." This diversification and recognition of outstanding teachers have just begun to take root in general education and must be considered in Jewish education as well. The position of master teacher or mentor would free a seasoned, reflective teacher from some of his or her classroom responsibilities in order to work with newcomers. With additional compensation, status, and the opportunity for further professional growth, veteran teachers would be shielded from burnout while novices would receive the one-on-one supervision that they deserve.

An infusion of funds, whether from Federations or family foundations, would encourage day schools to free up these teachers, allowing some of their more mundane tasks to be filled by novices or part-timers. Women like Nehama, who leave day school teaching for motherhood, might very well be lured back to the classroom on a part-time basis. As Biklen (1986) observes, choosing to bear and nurture children is not a sign of lack of commitment. Our concerns about professionalizing Jewish education must not shut out the people with "interrupted careers" (Biklen, p. 506) who can be utilized creatively to relieve those tapped to be mentor teachers until the part-timers are ready for classrooms of their own.

The Jewish community cannot expect the day school to be the Great White Hope of Jewish identity, cultural literacy, and survival. Day schools cannot possibly meet even the most modest of the expectations of the Jewish community until they undergo major changes. These changes must begin by imagining schools that prioritize caring for teachers—new hires as well as veterans. Day school leaders must nurture and support their teachers as well as their students. Heads of school cannot function like watchmaker gods, bringing on new hires, creating "teaching teams," and then retreating to let them flounder. They must advocate for their teachers, encouraging their boards to compensate their teachers fairly and to provide for their personal and professional growth.

A day school congress should be convened, bringing together teachers, administrators, teacher educators, funders, and policymakers to focus on the issues of retention and attrition. In order to create the faculties that they deserve, day schools must be able to count on the institutions that educate preservice teachers to provide their graduates with the highest level of Jewish cultural literacy, an exposure to the best models of pedagogy, and the richest field experience possible. Day schools must have the resources of community organizations and family foundations in order to do what they cannot do on their own: to create large-scale, comprehensive programs for mentoring novices, for meaningful professional development, for mentor training, and underwriting salaries and sabbaticals.

As I complete my portraits, I am struck by how often the word "vision" appears in today's conversations about Jewish education.

Day school education needs a vision of teacher induction that meets Houghton's objective: "to sustain all that is beautiful and glorious about being a teacher" (2001, p. 711). If not, day school teaching will continue to be known as a field that cannibalizes its young. If *Up the Down Staircase* is Bel Kaufman's tribute to the endurance of a young teacher's idealism, *Down the Up Staircase* is a sad reminder of its fragility.

Interview Protocols

From the first interview (1994):

1. Tell me a little about yourself and your family background. Can you give me a general characterization of your family? What are your parents' occupations? Number of siblings—ages, occupations? How long have you been living at your present home? Any large events that shaped the history and character of the family?
2. Would you describe your Jewish education, formal and informal? To what extent was your family involved in the Jewish community? Did your family belong to a synagogue? Describe. What, if any, was your experience in Jewish camps?
3. Tell me about yourself as a student. How do you view yourself as a student and learner? What sorts of learning environments did you experience at home? During your school years? As an undergraduate? What was your major as an undergraduate? How did you come to major in this field? What factors influenced your decision? What did your family think about this major? What were some of your best classes? Why? How would you characterize yourself as a student in these classes? Is this different from your other classes? What classes are you taking now? How do you feel about your preparation for these classes?
4. What made you want to become a teacher? Why a teacher in a Jewish school? Why a day school teacher? What occupations did you consider before you decided to become a day school teacher? Who or what might have inspired you in your decision to become a teacher? How, if at all, has your home life contributed to your decision? How, if at all, has camp contributed to your decision? How, if

at all, has your synagogue contributed to your decision? What sorts of career aspirations do you have? Which ones have you ruled out? Why? How are you able to finance your education?

5. What subjects do you want to teach and why? What grades and why? In what kind of Jewish day school and why? What are your expectations with regard to the students you will be teaching during this program? How do you see the school and classroom environments in which you will be working?

6. Would you please draw a concept map of the day school environment and walk me through it?

From the second interview (1996):

1. Catch up on bio. (Clarify any questions.)

2. Catch up on courses. What classes are you taking now? What are the classes like? What surprises you? What dismays you? What are you learning that you think is important? How is what you are doing connected to teaching? Can you give me an example of something you're doing being converted into a lesson?

3. Please review your student teaching experience. What do you think about your preparation for student teaching? What do you like about it? What might you improve?

4. As you come to the close of your master's program and approach graduation and the world of work, what do you think about the preservice preparation you've received?

5. What are your thoughts about day schools? How do you see the day school environment in which you are working?

6. Please draw a concept map of the day school environment and walk me through it. Is this what you envisioned before you began your student teaching? How does this map compare with your last map?

From the third interview (1997):

1. What did you do after graduation, and why did you decide to go that route?

2. What kind of year was it for you?

3. Looking back on your preservice education, how can we make that experience more effective for students like yourself?

4. What should an administrator expect in a newly hired day school teacher?
5. What do you expect to be doing next year?
6. Would you please draw me a concept map of a day school and then walk me through it? How does this map differ from the ones that preceded it?

From the fourth interview (1998):

1. Let's review your year. What came as a surprise to you as a new day school teacher? What did you feel well prepared for? What didn't you feel so well prepared for?
2. Could you have been better prepared for these surprises? If so, how?
3. What were the high points of the year? The low points?
4. What is your vision of a good day school?
5. What is your vision of good teaching in a day school?
6. What does a teacher need to know in order to succeed in a day school?
7. How do you plan to spend the next academic year?
8. Please draw a concept map of a day school. How does it compare with your previous drawings?

From the fifth interview (1999):

1. How have you changed as a teacher over the past year?
2. What did you bring to the profession in the way of your personal and cultural background that helped you? That hindered you?
3. When, over the course of the years you've spent in teaching, did you most feel like a teacher? Least like a teacher?
4. How, if at all, did your perceptions of the world of day school education change?
5. What are the challenges of being a day school educator?
6. How do the challenges of non-Jewish religious education compare with the challenges of day school education? And how do the challenges of religious education compare with the challenges of Jewish education?
7. Draw a concept map that best describes day school, and walk me through it.

8. How does this drawing compare with the others you have drawn?
9. Looking over these drawings, are there any patterns that you can see? What are they?
10. Is there anything else I should ask you?

After 1999–2000, I spoke to each of the teachers every year either in person, by telephone, or e-mail to catch up on their personal and professional lives. I did not use a structured interview format nor did I ask them to draw concept maps. Among the questions I asked were:

1. What is new, professionally and personally?
2. What gives you satisfaction in your work?
3. What drives you crazy?
4. Knowing what you now know about day schools, what advice would you give to yourself as a novice day school teacher?
5. How, if at all, has your thinking about day schools changed over time?

By 2001, all three had left day school teaching. I continued to speak with them through the summer of 2004. All three read the portraits that I wrote, corrected any errors of fact that I had made, and agreed with this representation of their experience.

References

Agenda. (2004). "Educator recruitment and retention." *Agenda: Jewish Education,* 17 (spring). New York: JESNA.

Antin, M. (1916/1965). "The lie." In *The Jewish caravan,* ed. L. Schwartz. New York: Schocken, 578–95.

Apple, M. W. (1990). *Ideology and curriculum.* New York: Routledge.

Aron, I. (1990). *Toward the professionalization of Jewish teaching.* New York: Commission on Jewish Education in North America.

Avi Chai Foundation. (2000). *1999 annual report.* New York: Avi Chai Foundation.

Ball, D. J. (1987). *The micro-politics of the school: Towards a theory of school organization.* London: Methuen.

Beinart, P. (1999). "The rise of Jewish schools." *The Atlantic Monthly, 284*(4), 21–22.

Biklen, S. (1986). "I have always worked: Elementary school teaching as a career." *Phi Delta Kappan, 67*(7), 504–8.

Borko, H., & Shavelson, R. J. (1983). "Speculations on teacher education: Recommendations from research on teachers' cognitions." *Journal of Education for Teaching, 9*(3), 210–24.

Bracey, G. W. (2002). *The war against America's public schools.* Saddle River, N.J.: Allyn & Bacon/Longman.

_____. (2003). *On the death of childhood and the destruction of public schools: The folly of today's education policies and practices.* Portsmouth, N.H.: Heinemann.

Bransford, J. D., Brown, A. L., & Cocking, R. R., eds. (2000). *How people learn: Brain, mind, experience, and school.* Washington, D.C.: National Academy Press.

Britzman, D. P. (1986). "Cultural myths in the making of a teacher: Biography and social structure in teacher education." *Harvard Educational Review, 56*(4), 442–56.

_____. (1991). *Practice makes practice: A critical study of learning to teach.* Albany: State University of New York Press.

Brodkin, K. (1998). *How Jews became white folks and what that says about race in America*. New Brunswick, N.J.: Rutgers University Press.

Bruner, J. (1986). *Actual minds, possible worlds*. Cambridge, Mass.: Harvard University Press.

Buchmann, M. (1987). "Teaching knowledge: The lights that teachers live by." *Oxford Review of Education, 13*(2), 151–64.

Buckley, F. J. (2000). *Team teaching: What, why, and how?* Thousand Oaks, Calif.: Sage.

Campbell, K. P. (1990–91). "Personal norms of experienced expert suburban high school teachers: Implications for selecting and retaining outstanding individuals." *Action in Teacher Education, 12*(4), 35–40.

Carnegie Forum on Education and the Economy. (1986). *A nation prepared: Teachers for the 21st century*. Washington, D.C.: Task Force on Teaching as a Profession.

Carter, K. (1990). "Teachers' knowledge and learning to teach." In *Handbook of research on teacher education*. New York: Macmillan, 291–310.

_____, Cushing, K., Sabers, D., Stein, P., & Berliner, D. (1988). "Expert-novice differences in perceiving and processing visual classroom information." *Journal of Teacher Education, 39*(3), 25–31.

Clandinin, D. J., & Connelly, F. M. (1996). "Teachers' professional knowledge landscapes: Teacher stories, stories of teachers, school stories, stories of schools." *Educational Researcher, 25*(3), 24–30.

Clark, C. M., & Yinger, R. J. (1977). "Research on teacher thinking." *Curriculum Inquiry, 7*(4), 279–304.

Cliburn, J. W., Jr. (1990). "Concept maps to promote meaningful learning." *Journal of College Science Teaching, 19*(4), 212–17.

Cohen, R. M. (1991). *A lifetime of teaching: Portraits of five veteran high school teachers*. New York: Teachers College Press.

Cohen, S. M., & Eisen, A. M. (2000). *The Jew within: Self, family, and community in America*. Bloomington: Indiana University Press.

Copeland, W. D., Birmingham, C., De Meulle, L., D'Emidio-Caston, M., & Natal, B. (1994). "Making meaning in classrooms: An investigation of cognitive processes in aspiring teachers, experienced teachers, and their peers." *American Educational Research Journal, 31*(1), 166–96.

Curran, B., & Goldrick, L. (2002). *Mentoring and supporting new teachers*. Issue Brief. Washington, D.C.: National Governors' Association Center for Best Practices.

Cushing, K. S., Sabers, D. S., & Berliner, D. C. (1992). "Olympic gold: Investigations of expertise in teaching." *Educational Horizons, 70*(3), 108–14.

Deshler, D. (1990). "Conceptual mapping: Drawing charts of the mind." In *Fostering critical reflection in adulthood*, ed. J. Mezirow and Associates. San Francisco: Jossey-Bass, 336–53.

Donaldson, M. L., & Poon, B., eds. (1999). *Reflections of first-year teachers on school culture: Questions, hopes, and challenges.* San Francisco: Jossey-Bass.

Drake, S. M. (1993). *Planning integrated curriculum.* Alexandria, Va.: ASCD.

Durkheim, E. (1973). *Moral education: A study in the theory and application of the sociology of education.* New York: Free Press.

Elbaz, F. (1983). *Teacher thinking: A study of practical knowledge.* New York: Nichols.

———. (1991). "Research on teachers' knowledge: The evolution of a discourse." *Journal of Curriculum Studies, 23*(1), 1–19.

Fausto-Sterling, A. (1985). *Myths of gender.* New York: Basic Books.

Feiman-Nemser, S. (1983). "Learning to teach." In *Handbook of teaching and policy,* ed. L. S. Shulman & G. Sykes. New York: Longman, 150–70.

———. (2001). "Helping novices to teach: Lessons from an exemplary support teacher." *Journal of Teacher Education, 52*(1), 17–30.

———. (2003). "What new teachers need to learn." *Educational Leadership, 60*(8), 25–29.

Fenstermacher, G. (1994). "The knower and the known: The nature of knowledge." In *Review of research in education,* ed. L. Darling-Hammond. Washington, D.C.: American Educational Research Association, 20, 3–56.

Fishman, S. B. (2000). *American culture and Jewish life.* New York: State University of New York Press.

Friedlaender, I. (1907/2004). "The problem of Judaism in America." *Conservative Judaism, 56*(special supplement), 6–19.

Geffen, R. M. (2004). "Is the dawn of the Jews the dusk of Judaism?" *Conservative Judaism, 56*(special supplement), 27–34.

Goodman, R. L. (2002). "Insights on retention from Jewish educational research." *Jewish Educational News, 23*(3), 25–28.

Grossman, P. L., & Richert, A. E. (1996). "Building capacity and commitment for leadership in preservice teacher education." *Journal of School Leadership, 6,* 202–10.

Hansen, D. (1995). *The call to teach.* New York: Teachers College Press.

Heller, D. A. (2004). *Teachers wanted: Attracting and retaining good teachers.* Alexandria, Va.: ASCD.

Himmelfarb, H. S. (1975). "Jewish education for naught: Educating the culturally deprived Jewish child." *Analysis* 51 (September). Institute for Jewish Policy Planning and Research of the Synagogue Council of America.

The Holmes Group. (1986). *Tomorrow's teachers: A report of the Holmes Group.* East Lansing, Mich.: Holmes Group.

Houghton, P. (2001). "Sustaining teachers' health and well-being." *Phi Delta Kappan, 83*(5), 706–11.

Hunter, J. D. (2001). *The death of character: On the moral education of America's children.* New York: Basic Books.

Ingall, C. K. (1997). *Maps, metaphors and mirrors: Moral education in middle schools.* Greenwich, Conn.: Ablex.

———, & Malkus, M. (2001). "Negotiating the borderlands: Implementing an integrated curricular unit in a Jewish day high school." *Journal of Jewish Education, 67*(1–2), 36–45.

Ingersoll, R. M., & Smith, T. M. (2003). "The wrong solution to the teacher shortage." *Educational Leadership, 60*(8), 30–38.

Jackson, P. (1990). *Life in classrooms.* New York: Teachers College Press.

JERRI e-Newsletter. (2004). "Jewish educator recruitment and retention initiative" (May 21). Retrieved December 30, 2004, from http://209.35.238.38/enews/jerri.

Johnson, M. (1989). "Embodied knowledge." *Curriculum Inquiry, 19*(3), 361–77.

Johnson, S. M., & Birkeland, S. E. (2003). "Pursuing a 'sense of success': New teachers explain their career decisions." *American Educational Research Journal, 40*(3), 581–617.

Kagan, D. M. (1992). "Professional growth among preservice and beginning teachers." *Review of Educational Research, 62*(2), 129–69.

Kaufman, B. (1970). *Up the down staircase.* Englewood Cliffs, N.J.: Prentice-Hall.

Kelner, S., Rabkin, M., Saxe, L., & Sheingold, C. (2004). "Recruiting and retaining a professional work force for the Jewish community: A review of existing research." Waltham, Mass.: Brandeis University. Retrieved December 27, 2004, from http://register.birthrightisrael.org/files/RRLR.pdf.

Kilbourn, B., & Roberts, G. (1991). "May's first year: Conversations with a mentor." *Teachers College Record, 93*(2), 252–64.

Knowles, J. G. (1988). "A beginning teacher's experience: Reflections on becoming a teacher." *Language Arts, 65*(7), 702–12.

Kohl, H. (1998). *The discipline of hope: Learning from a lifetime of teaching.* New York: Simon and Schuster.

Krebs, A. (2001). "Eudora Welty, a lyrical master of the short story, is dead at 92." *New York Times* (July 24), A1, C22.

Lawrence-Lightfoot, S. (1983). *The good high school: Portraits of character and culture.* New York: Basic Books.

———, & Hoffman Davis, J. (1997). *The art and science of portraiture.* San Francisco: Jossey-Bass.

Levin, B. B., & Ammon, P. (1996). "A longitudinal study of the development of teachers' pedagogical conceptions: The case of Ron." *Teacher Education Quarterly, 23*(4), 5–25.

Lortie, D. C. (1975). *Schoolteacher: A sociological study.* Chicago: University of Chicago Press.

Malkus, M. (2001). "Portraits of curricular integration in Jewish day schools." Ph.D. diss., Jewish Theological Seminary.

Markowitz, R. J. (1993). *My daughter the teacher: Jewish teachers in the New York City schools.* New Brunswick, N.J.: Rutgers University Press.

Maslach, C. (1982). *Burnout: The cost of caring.* Englewood Cliffs, N.J.: Prentice-Hall.

Menand, L. (2001). "False fronts." *The New Yorker* (July 23), 78–80.

Mintz, A. (1997). "The divided fate of Hebrew and Hebrew culture at the Seminary." In *Tradition renewed: A history of the Jewish Theological Seminary of America,* ed. J. Wertheimer. New York: Jewish Theological Seminary, 2:81–112.

National Jewish Population Survey (NJPS). (1991). Kosmin, B., Goldstein, S., Waksberg, J., Lerer, N., Keysar, A., and Scheckner, J. *Highlights of the 1990 National Jewish Population Survey.* New York: Council of Jewish Federations.

Ness, M. (2001). "Lessons of a first-year teacher." *Phi Delta Kappan, 83*(5), 700–701.

Noddings, N. (1992). *The challenge to care in schools: An alternative approach to education.* New York: Teachers College Press.

Novak, J. D. (1990). "Concept maps and vee diagrams: Two metacognitive tools to facilitate meaningful learning." *Instructional Science, 19*(1), 29–52.

O'Donnell, E. (2004). "Left in the chalkdust: Blackboard brain drain." *Harvard Magazine, 107*(1), 19–20.

Paley, V. G. (2002). *White teacher.* 3rd ed. Cambridge, Mass.: Harvard University Press.

Palmer, P. (1998–99). "Evoking the spirit in public education." *Educational Leadership, 56*(4), 6–11.

Peerless, S. (2002). "Mentoring revisited." *Jewish Education News, 23*(3), 66–67.

PEJE. (2000). *Day schools: Transforming the Jewish future: A Report of the partnership for excellence in Jewish education* (September). Boston: PEJE.

Perez, K., Swain, C., & Hartsough, C. S. (1997). "An analysis of practices used to support new teachers." *Teacher Education Quarterly, 24*(2), 41–52.

Pollak, J. P., & Mills, R. A. (1997). "True collaboration: Building and maintaining successful teams." *Schools in the Middle, 6*(5), 28–32.

Pomson. A. (2000). "Who's a Jewish teacher? A narrative inquiry into general studies teachers in Jewish day schools." *Journal of Jewish Communal Service, 77*(1), 56–63.

_____. (2001). "Making the best of the worst of times: Thinking of schools as vehicles of meaning for teachers." *Jewish Education News, 33*(3), 59–61.

Public Education Network (PEN). (2003). *The voice of the new teacher* (fall). Retrieved December 27, 2004, from http://www.publiceducation.org/pdf/Publications/Teacher_Quality/Voice_of_the_New_Teacher.pdf.

Rose, L. C., & Gallup, A. M. (2002). "The 34th annual Phi Delta Kappa Gallup poll of the public's attitudes toward the public schools." *Phi Delta Kappan, 84*(1), 41–56.

Rowley, J. B. (1999). "The good mentor." *Educational Leadership, 56*(8), 20–22.

Ryan, K. (1986). *The induction of new teachers.* Bloomington, Ind.: Phi Delta Kappa Educational Foundation.

_____, ed. (1992). *The roller coaster year: Essays by and for beginning teachers.* New York: HarperCollins.

Schaap, E., with assistance from A. Ackerman. (2002). "Three CAJE surveys: Number of educators, benefits available to CAJE members, and recruitment and retention facts." *Jewish Education News, 23*(3), 12–16.

Schamber, S. (1999). "Surviving team teaching's good intentions." *Education Digest, 64*(8), 18–23.

Scheffler, I. (1995). *Teachers of my youth.* Dordrecht, Netherlands: Kluwer Academic Publishers, 1995.

Scherer, M. (2001). "Improving the quality of the teaching force: A conversation with David C. Berliner." *Educational Leadership, 58*(8), 6–10.

Schick, M. (2000). *A census of Jewish day schools in the United States.* New York: Avi Chai Foundation.

Schoen, D. A. (1983). *The reflective practitioner: How professionals think in action.* New York: Basic Books.

Shulman, L. S. (1987). "Knowledge and teaching: Foundations of the new reform." *Harvard Educational Review, 57*(1), 1–22.

Sikes, P. (1997). *Parents who teach: Stories from home and from school.* London: Cassell.

Smith, M. K. (2001). "Peter Senge and the learning organization." In *The encyclopedia of informal education.* Retrieved December 30, 2004, from www.infed.org/thinkers/senge.htm.

Smith, T. M., & Ingersoll, R. M. (2004). "Effects of induction and mentoring on teacher turnover." *American Educational Research Journal, 41*(3), 681–714.

Stark, S. (1991). "Toward an understanding of the beginning-teacher experience: Curricular insights for teacher education." *Journal of Curriculum and Supervision, 6*(4), 294–311.

Sternberg, R. J., & Horvath, J. A. (1995). "A prototype view of expert teaching." *Educational Researcher, 24*(6), 9–17.

Stone, B. (1987). "Why beginning teachers fail—and what you can do about it." *Principal, 67*(1), 33–35.

Tye, B. B., & O'Brien, L. (2002). "Why are experienced teachers leaving the profession?" *Phi Delta Kappan, 84*(1), 24–32.

Wadsworth, D. (2001). "Why new teachers choose to teach." *Educational Leadership, 58*(8), 24–28.

Weinstein, C. S. (1989). "Teacher education students' preconceptions of teaching." *Journal of Teacher Education, 40*(2), 53–60.

Weiss, B. J., ed. (1982). *American education and the European immigrant 1840–1940.* Urbana: University of Illinois Press.

Wertheimer, J. (1999). "Jewish education in the United States: Recent trends and issues." In *American Jewish year book, 1999.* Bloomsberg, Pa.: Haddon Craftsmen, 3–115.

Williams, J. S. (2003). "Why great teachers stay." *Educational Leadership*, 60(8), 71–74.

Wilson, S. M. (1991). "Parades of facts, stories of the past: What do novice history teachers need to know?" In *Teaching academic subjects to diverse learners*, ed. M. M. Kennedy. New York: Teachers College Press, 99–116.

Winter, N. H. (1966). *Jewish education in a pluralist society: Samson Benderly and Jewish education in the United States*. New York: New York University Press.

Zeichner, K., & Tabachnick, B. R. (1985). "The development of teacher perspective: Social strategies and institutional control in the socialization of beginning teachers." *Journal of Education for Teaching*, 11(1), 1–25.

Zeldin, M., & Lee, S., eds. (1995). *Touching the future: Mentoring and the Jewish professional*. Los Angeles: Hebrew Union College–Jewish Institute of Religion.

Zimmerman, S. (2003). "Stubbornness and the kindness of strangers." *Educational Leadership*, 60(8), 76–77.

Zmuda, A., Kuklis, R., & Kline, E. (2004). *Transforming schools: Creating a culture of continuous improvement*. Alexandria, Va.: ASCD.

Index

An index is a labor of love. This index is dedicated to the memory of two passionate Jewish educators, Lori Rosen and Rabbi Sol Tanenzapf, *zikhronam livrakhah.*—L.R.

vocation, choice of
   personal value system and 41

W
Wadsworth, D. 108, 120, 133
Weinstein, C. S. 17, 28, 31, 94, 103
Weiss, B. J. 5
Wertheimer, J. 6–7
William Davidson Graduate School of
   Jewish Education. *See* Jewish
   Theological Seminary of America
Williams, J. S. 11, 35, 41, 108, 135
Wilson, S. M. 9

Winter, N. H. 7
women's professions 2, 137

Y
Yinger, R. J. 26
young teachers. *See* novice teachers

Z
Zeichner, K. 92
Zeldin, M. 107
Zimmerman, S. 110
Zmuda, A. 129, 133